R. Gupta's®

SUCCESS
in
INTERVIEW

A PATH FINDER FOR STUDENTS

RAMESH PUBLISHING HOUSE, New Delhi

Published by:
O.P. Gupta *for* Ramesh Publishing House

Admin. Office:
12-H, New Daryaganj Road, Opp. Officers' Mess,
New Delhi-110002 ① 23261567, 23275224, 23275124

E-mail: info@rameshpublishinghouse.com
Website: www.rameshpublishinghouse.com

Showroom:
● Balaji Market, Nai Sarak, Delhi-6 ① 23253720, 23282525
● 4457, Nai Sarak, Delhi-6, ① 23918938

Book Code: R-1330

7th Revised Edition : 1710

ISBN: 978-93-5012-021-7

HSN Code: 49011010

Preface

Interview is a kind of sale and purchase process. Candidate tries to sell his/her knowledge, experience, personality. In short he/she sells himself/herself in interview, and an interviewer tries to purchase a candidate for his institution or firm.

Interview is the part of career through which one can achieve his/her goal or destination. There are many essential things for an interview to which, a candidate should give his/her proper attention and make preparation for these things to get success.

We all face the interview from getting admission in nursery class to getting a job for career. As we grow up, we understand the social and practical norms along with our expectations. And for fulfilment of desires and expectations we use our study, qualification, work experience, personality, merit etc., all the things we have for getting a desired job. But some of us have nervousness, fears etc., so that despite all the best qualities, they do not succeed in an interview.

We are trying to give brief knowledge about various interview tools and techniques and some samples of different kinds of interviews, so that candidates may be benefitted as per their choices and desires.

Hope, it will prove valuable to interviewees and for those candidates who are preparing for a job in their career.

All the best to all our readers!!

—Publisher

Contents

Chapter 1

An Introduction

The word 'interview' is made up with two words 'inter' and 'view', which means between two or more and to see gradually. So, an interview means interaction between two or more people face to face. The main aim behind an interview is to determine the ability and eligibility of a candidate for a particular job. It is the final hurdle for a candidate by which his/her personal qualities such as intelligence, manner, attitude, hobbies, over all personalities are evaluated. It is an important stage before selection for any job. So, we can say that an interview is the scale to measure the personality appropriate for job, and the organization.

Winning is an event, but being a winner is a spirit.

To win, one will have to understand the spirit of deserving something before getting it. The mantra for success in top most examination is to cultivate the real 'joy of learning' as a pre-condition for any learning to start impacting one's mind.

The most important part of the interview is "the person". Everything else that goes on in an interview is peripheral or secondary. Talking about oneself is not easy for any one in such a situation. Yet, that is what precisely one is required to do in an interview. One's achievements, interests and visions are what the person must be ready to talk about in a clear-headed manner. An interview is a celebration of "the person" from start to finish.

Thus, an interview is the final step in the selection process where face to face communication takes place and impressions are formed of the personality, values and forms of mind towards life of the applicant. Interview is more of a process of discussion and conversation than interrogation to find out the positive and negative traits of the personality of the candidate.

Phases of Interview

The whole interview process can be divided into four phases:

(*i*) **Phase One:** When the interviewee enters the interview hall, he/she greets the interviewers and is asked to have a seat. The interviewers observe the way of entering, greeting, facial expression, overall look and external body language. Actually the first phase of interview marks the very first impression which is most important for further proceedings.

(*ii*) **Phase Two:** After primary suitability, intelligence, attitude and approach, working style, organisational capabilities, hobbies etc are judged by the interviewers to ascertain the fitness of interviewee in respect to the responsibilities and duties of the job. They also judge; how he/she reacts to the questions or handles a specific problem or solve a specific problem.

(*iii*) **Phase Three:** In this crucial phase, interviewers see the potentional of interviewee in achieving the goals of the organisation. They want to see that, if the interviewee will be able to associate with the company for a fairly long term or not.

(*iv*) **Phase Four:** It is the final phase where all the formalities are discussed and interviewers give the opportunity to ask the questions from them to take any decision. It is the phase where interviewee makes the last but indelible impression on the employer by demonstrating his willingness and interest in the organisation.

Thus, the interview is the process by which interviewers are more keen in knowing the real persona in you and bring the best out of you.

OOO

Preparation

Before the Interview

A job interview may be the most intense and dynamic situation that one encounters in their career. So, one ought to prepare adequately for success at the interview. For proper preparation one should—

- Do self analysis to know one's strengths and weaknesses.
- Understand the knowledge and skills that he/she possess.
- Find out how relevant his/her competence is to the job.
- Find out how one would use it for performing the required duties.
- Gather information about the history, functional and developmental plan of the organisation
- Visualize the role one could play in the organisation's growth and development.

Apart from all these things the interviewee should know the entire selection process and various steps adopted by the recruiting organisation in screening and selecting candidates. It is important for candidates to understand the purpose of an interview so that he/she is able to prepare for it in a more methodological and scientific manner. In an interview all the aspects of knowledge and personality are examined by the interviewer, so a candidate must be aware of happenings in the environment in which he/she lives, works, plays and tackles all the daily problems of surviving.

Biodata or Resume

For preparation for an interview, the very first step is to prepare a detailed biographical data to oneself whether he/she is fresher or experienced. Biodata or Resume is firstly sent with the application for vacancy of the job. Now-a-days some corporates and Government offices prescribe a biodata form which is filled by the candidate at the interview venue before some time of interview. Candidate should prepare the biodata very carefully, because each member has a brief resume of the candidate's qualifications before him and they ask questions through resume also, so a candidate must be aware of what he/she has mentioned in the resume. The appearance of the candidate and his/her biodata constitutes a stimulus to the members of the boards, who react to the past record of the candidate, as well as to the answers given by him.

A general biodata or resume contains each and every information about candidate's name, address, date of birth, marital status, academic records, details of experiences, extra-curricular activities, hobbies, willingness and name of the applied post.

It is a common experience that a large number of candidates belonging to lower middle class families have to do part-time job as clerk, cashier, teacher even as tutor or carrying the newspaper or magazines in student life. Candidates are often reluctant to mention these at all, thinking that this may prejudice the board against them. This is a totally erroneous impression. Each and every work is honourable in order to earn an honest livelihood. It shows grit, determination, capacity to rough out and such sterling qualities. It helps the interview boards to find out whether the candidate is telling the truth or not.

Candidates should not hesitate to mention any such work experience that they had in past or which they have at present. Interviewers look on favourably towards candidates who struggle through thick and thin and try to stand on their own feet. Self-made persons are always considered and appraised by all. Each and everything mentioned by candidate in his/her resume reflects the image of candidate. So, be careful and keep honesty in preparation of biodata.

Sample Curriculum Vitae

(*a*) Information Technology

SANTHOSH B.
Sankar reddy,
#5588, Konappa Nagar
Electronic City,
Bangalore-560100
Mobile No: 21-99999999
E-mail: ssss@ssssl.com

OBJECTIVE

Seeking a position to utilize my skills and abilities in the Information Technology Industry that offers Professional growth while being resourceful, innovative and flexible.

EDUCATION:

Maharaja Engineering College - May, 20...
B.TECH (Information Technology)
Percentage scored: 67%

Shri Ganga Higher Secondary School - March, 20...
Percentage scored: 88%

Govt Boys Higher Secondary School - March, 20...
Percentage scored: 68%

TECHNICAL EXPERIENCE:

- Languages: C, C, CORE JAVA, VB 6.0,UNIX Shell Scripts, HTML .
- Platforms: Windows xp/2000/7/8, Vista NT, Red Hat Linux (9.0, ES, WS)
- Concepts: Networking, Operating Systems

CERTIFICATIONS:

- Red Hat Certified Engineer (RHCE) -Enterprise Linux 4 # 1114006719821418
- Expertise in: Installing Red Hat Linux Configuring Servers (DNS, FTP, NFS, NIS, SAMBA, APACHE, DHCP, MAIL), Troubleshooting, User Permissions (LVM)
- Brain-bench certified Linux Assessment #T20110714001A

PROJECT EXPERIENCE:

1. Final Semester Project as Part of the B.TECH Curriculum. Project Name: "Integrated Java Based Web server" Description: The powerful web server that enhances java based applications and provides authentication.

MINI PROJECTS:

1. Creating a Manual Dictionary in V.B. 6.
2. Deleting the files concurrently using shell scripts

ELECTIVES TAKEN:

Linux Servers, Distributed Systems

OTHER ACTIVITIES & HOBBIES:

- Organizing various Cultural Programmes & Won Prizes.
- Reading E-books
- Net-surfing

PERSONAL DETAILS:

Name: Santhosh B.

Age & DOB: 21 years, 21-06-19...
Sex: Male
Marital Status: Single
Nationality: Indian
Permanent Address: 18/120, Guruswamy Nagar,
V.L. Road,
Peelamedu,
Coimbatore-04
Tamil Nadu, India
Contact Number: 0111-11112027

Languages Known: English, Tamil

Declaration

I hereby declare that the above written particulars are true to the best of my knowledge and belief.

(SANTHOSH B.)

(b) Academic

John Smith
Street, City, State, Zip
Phone: 555-555-5555
Cell: 555-666-6666
email@email.com

OBJECTIVE:
To apply for the position of Assistant Professor, Psychology.

EDUCATION:
Ph.D., Psychology, University of Minnesota, 20...
Concentrations: Psychology, Community Psychology

DISSERTATION:

A Study of Learning Disabled Children in a Low Income Community

M.A., Psychology, University at Albany, 20...
Concentrations: Psychology, Special Education
Thesis: Communication Skills of
Learning Disabled Children

B.A, Psychology, California State University,
Long Beach, CA, 20...

EXPERIENCE:

• Instructor, 20...-20...
University of Minnesota
Course: Psychology in the Classroom

• Teaching Assistant, 20...-20...
University at Albany
Courses: Special Education, Learning Disabilities

RESEARCH SKILLS:

Extensive knowledge of SPSSX and
SAS statistical programs.

PRESENTATIONS:

Smith John (20...). The behaviour of learning disabled adolescents in the classrooms. Paper presented at the Psychology Conference at the University of Minnesota.

PUBLICATIONS:

Smith, John (20...). The behaviour of learning disabled adolescents in the classroom. Journal of Educational Psychology, 120-125.

GRANTS AND FELLOWSHIPS:

- RDB Grant (University of Minnesota Research Grant, 20...), $2000
- Workshop Grant (for ASPA meeting in New York, 20...), $1500

AWARDS AND HONOURS:

- Treldar Scholar, 20...
- Academic Excellent Award, 20...

SKILLS AND QUALIFICATIONS:

- Microsoft Office, Internet
- Programming ability in C++ and PHP
- Fluent in German, French and Spanish

REFERENCES:

Excellent references available upon request.

The resume and the application are the things that create your first impression in the prospective organisation. These things help the employer in shortlisting the candidates for interview.

○○○

Chapter 3

About Job

A candidate must know about the desired job which he/she wants and what the employer requires, what are the priorities and what the employer prefers. As an interviewee one has to sell his/herself so he/she should know that for what he/she has to sell himself/herself and whether that is suitable or not. The interviewers also evaluate one's skills as per the job requirement, so one should have the basic, technical and appropriate knowledge about the applied job.

About Organisation/Employer

After knowing about job, the candidate should know about the organisation, and the employer. There are generally two types of organisation small and large. On the basis of one's own objectives, skills and wishes, candidate should choose the organisation. A large organisation offers its employees a great sense of security and identity, but it can produce the feelings of insignificance because each employee feels that he is a cog in the wheel of a specialized machine. A large organisation does not offer its employees breadth of experience especially in the initial years of their employment.

A small organization provides a more informal climate as it does not have many narrow functional area. Here an employee is able to gain greater breadth of experience. It depends upon candidate what he/she chooses. Some medium sized organisations are also there in which there are positive combinations of those two.

It is very essential for a candidate to do relevant research about the company/organisation and the applied job. Research gives information and knowledge. A candidate can reply a number of questions fired at him/her during the interview with the help of research. It shows one's willingness and sincerity to join the particular position. Questions like—Why do you like to join this company? or How you are suitable for it? or How could you be able to face the challenges entailing to the position you have applied for?—are asked to know one's preparation and knowledge about the company/employer. The more, one knows about the organisation, position, products and about the other similar and competitive company, the chances will be more to success in the interview.

One should try to know about—

- Business of the employer
- Duties and responsibilities of the job
- Skills and experience required by the employer
- Various business database and industry news
- Company's operations for the last three years
- Planning of the company for the year ahead
- Trends of the turnover, profit, mergers etc of the company
- Company's important clients
- Global market, quality control and improvement, profitability of the company
- Competitors or rivals of the company, etc.

A candidate can get the desired information from—

- The website of company
- Sales brochures
- Annual reports and accounts
- Customer newsletters
- In-house or trade magazines
- Products of the company
- Any person who is working in the company.

When a candidate feels familiar to the company he/she will be more comfortable in the interview. A good quality research and thinking makes the candidate capable and eligible for the job and company.

○○○

Chapter 4

Ingredients for Success

> *To overcome the stress of interview a candidate should adopt the philosophy that "you win some, you lose some". Do not take things too seriously or emotionally. One might be excellent in academic record or a good performer, but there are chances that he/she may fail in an all important "job interview". A successful interview or success in interview means getting a job offer. There are some ingredients for success in the interview.*

Confidence

Confidence stems from thorough preparation and consistent endeavour. Like Arjuna, the great warrior of Mahabharata, one should become objective oriented. It helps a great deal in sharpening the intellect and making one bold. Always consider that you are born to succeed, because such thoughts contribute to your success.

Self confidence is deep-rooted in experience, knowledge and practice. Confident candidates perform well at interview. When a candidate does research and knows about the company, the job etc., he/she will be confident and comfortable in the interview. To develop the confidence one should—

- Be able to talk concisely about him/herself.
- Express key qualities and skills in a saleable manner.
- Be open-minded and honest throughout the interview.
- Think on his/her feet and express in business manner.
- Talk and answer in clear voice without any nervousness.
- Not afraid of the answer whatever it may be.

Keep in mind, always, that only they can conquer who believe they can. The overriding importance of self-confidence and the strong conviction that one would reach the goal, whatever be the hurdles and distractions, are the stepping stones to success. What is required is indomitable faith that looks through all minor failures, self-doubts and occasional bursts of pessimism. When such a dogged faith permeates your thinking, words and deeds, nothing can stop you from grabbing the prized position you are looking for. Those who have climbed up the ladder of success have never been disheartened by a false step here or there, but the iron resolve to climb up has helped them reach the summit of fame and success.

How to Build up your Self-confidence

Self-confidence can be developed in following ways—

- Fear robs you of courage and cripples your reasoning power. You need courage and confidence to overcome fear.
- Success comes to you only through your will-power to succeed.
- A positive attitude is pre-requisite for self-confidence.
- Develop your mental attitude in such a way that you have no fear and you can do it without any problem.
- Try to know your weakness and overcome them.

Positive Attitude

It is a mental attitude that admits into the mind thoughts, words and images that are conducive to growth, expansion and success. A positive mind anticipates happiness, joy, health and a successful outcome of every situation and action. When the attitude is positive we entertain pleasant feelings and constructive images, and see in our mind's eye what we really want to happen. This brings brightness to the eyes, more energy and happiness. The whole being broadcasts goodwill, happiness and success. Even the health is affected in a beneficial way. We walk tall and the voice is more powerful. Our body language shows the way we feel inside.

Positive and negative thinking are both contagious. All of us affect, in one way or another, the people we meet. This happens instinctively and on a subconscious level, through thoughts and feelings transference, and through body language. People see our aura and are affected by our thoughts, and vice-versa.

Negative thoughts, words and attitude bring up negative and unhappy mood and actions. When the mind is negative, toxins are released into the blood, which cause more unhappiness and negativity. This is the way to failure, frustration and disappointment. Once a negative thought enters our mind, we have to be aware of it and endeavour to replace it with a constructive one. The negative thought will try again to enter our mind and then we have to replace it again with a positive one. Persistence will eventually teach our mind to think positively and ignore negative thoughts. In order to turn the mind towards the positive, inner work and training are required. Attitude and thoughts do not change overnight. So be optimistic and active, hope for the sky and we will learn to fly with joy.

The main obstacles in the way of success are tardiness and lack of will power. Strong and affirmative will power comes from inner positive attitude. So, the positive attitude is indeed the most crucial plank for success. If the candidate has to overcome all the negative feelings, he needs to mould such a frame of mind that inspires confidence not only in himself but in others who are there to help him come out with the best in him.

Dressing Sense

Knowing what to wear for an interview is very important because dress reflects one's personality with the help of colour, style and design. One should specially take care of colour. It should not be of bright colour. It should be of sober colour which can make a viable first impression.

Though no one is ever selected because of the dress, it can be the cause of failure. Whether a candidate is man or woman, his/her clothes should give a professional look. Costly and expensive clothing and accessories do not make a good impression so it should be avoided. The dress should be elegantly suited to the candidate.

Body Language

Various postures, figures, facial expressions, voice, eyes, eyebrows etc. reflect one's personality, vitality and confidence. It all comes within body language, which is the most important aspect of an interview and makes the first impression. Various reflections of body language may be positive or negative. Positive effect may bring success and negative effect may ruin the career.

Some persons look puzzled or confused while speaking and unknowingly entwine their face in a strange way. Smiling with open lips, running tongue over the teeth, clearing throat, hands touching the nose or ear, running fingers through hair, biting on pen or finger rotating fingers, crossed arms, darting eyes, looking down when speaking or answering—are negative gestures which may affect one's interview or even job-career. Most of these gestures indicate anxiousness/nervousness and lack of confidence and sincerity.

The fear of what may go wrong, ranges from drying up one's throat to soaking the interviewers by spilling tea or coffee. If one can minimize the likelihood of things going wrong, fear will automatically be minimized or removed. The best way to overcome the fear is to rehearse as thoroughly as one can, the whole process of interview, with the help of friends or family members. Nervousness is quite natural phenomena which can not only be reduced, but almost finished, by doing some exercise and taking care of some natural things. For this, one should :

- think about answers to the likely questions and the tough ones
- practise in front of mirror
- rehearse opening greetings
- try the clothes in advance
- imagine the worst questions, consider every possible embarrassment one can face and plan for it with a cool mind.

The more one is prepared the less he/she feels fear and the less nervousness. To keep a smile on lips gives relaxation and makes environment easy.

The worst one can do to block the prospects of success at the interview, or any situation in life is to grow nervous. Think positively and banish all kinds of fear. Imagine that you are a born winner.

Communication Skills

Power of expression depends on communication skills which play a very important role in getting success in an interview. Despite of handsome personality with gentle manners, depth in subject knowledge, technical skills, good communication skills are very necessary for any candidate. Presenting the knowledge and skills in a convincing and rational manner is a big thing and it turns the carrer in one's favour. In an interview, interviewer wants to know a lot of details about the candidate, and wants to check his/her ability and manner to explain all things about his/herself.

There are six C's of effective communication skill—**Clarity, Completeness, Conciseness, Confidence, Correctness** and **Courteousness.**

All these things must be there in an interviewee, so that he/she conveys all the things smoothly. A good candidate should stay within limits, avoid talking irrelevantly. One should:

- Speak in an audible tone, neither be too quick nor be too slow.
- Be succinct and specific.
- Reveal the positive points and assets in the best possible manner during the interview.
- Just state the facts.
- Lay emphasis or lower the tone over the words where necessary.

- Never speak in dragging or mumbling voice.
- Be a good listener and judge what the interviewer wants from the candidate.
- Speak with confidence and look into the eyes of the interviewer with confidence.
- Make a request if he/she in unable to hear or understand the questions asked by the interviewer.

To communicate effectively a candidate should use words which are well understood and have powerful touch. Success in interviews depends a lot on your vocabulary and the ability of presentation. The words used by a candidate give an impression as if he/she is a little more intelligent and a little more informed than the other candidate.

Hobbies and Interests

Some hobbies and interests demonstrate the relevant skills, which can be mentioned on the resume, though most of the expert advise, not to mention hobbies, because it affect rather if a candidate does not give satisfactory answer regarding hobbies. It is considered a filler, which makes resume more lengthy. Sometimes it gives benefit to some candidate, when it is matched with interviewer's own hobby, so we can say that hobbies and interests are not the most important ingredients but least. Success depends on skills, intelligence, motivation, overall personality— which is an indefinable thing, a strange force that has power over souls of men.

Question-Answer Drill

Question-answer session is most important phase of interview, where a candidate is evaluated by his/her relevant answers, the manner of giving answers, thoughts and intellectual skills. An interviewer evaluates the candidate's personal abilities, temperament, and ability to work with team. The very purpose of the question-answer session is to find out in clear terms the positive and negative traits of the personality of the candidate.

These questions have great value for the employer and employee both. A candidate should reply all the questions with confidence, and understand well the idea behind the questions appropriately.

Some common questions that have great value behind them are:

(*a*) Tell us something about yourself.

Value behind

- What type of person are you?
- Whether you can relate your background with the job?
- What are your past experience, achievements and knowledge?

(*b*) Why should we hire you?

Value behind

- Whether you are the right/appropriate person or not?

(*c*) What do you know about our company/organisation?

Value behind

- What do you know about the company?
- What do you know about the applied job?
- Find seriousness for the job.

(*d*) What motivates you?

Value behind

- What are your priorities—concerned with salary, perks or reward?
- What are your expectations from the employer?

(*e*) Why did you leave your last job? or

Why do you want to leave your present job?

Value behind

- If you are fired from your job?
- If any problem with your job?
- If any expectation with that employer?

(*f*) What prompted you to apply for this job?

Value behind

- Do you really know the job profile?
- Whether you are interested in the applied job?

(*g*) Why have you been out of work so long?

Value behind

- What have you been doing during the gap?
- Are you not capable to handle the job?

(*h*) Who has inspired you and why?

Value behind

- Who is your ideal in the industry?
- Do you know about the top figures in the industry?

(*i*) When do you lose temper?

Value behind

- What is your temperament?
- How do you behave in odd circumstances?

(*j*) What part of your previous/present job you found most critical?

Value behind

- When you feel difficulties in job?
- What is your suitability for the job?

(*k*) Are you comfortable with a younger or a female colleague?

Value behind

- If you have any prejudices against the female or younger colleagues?
- Have you any problem with any senior/junior?

(*l*) Describe a challenging moment in past job?

Value behind

- How does a candidate face a challenge?
- If there are any hidden personality traits of the candidate.

(*m*) How do you express 'Success'?

Value behind

- The thought about success.
- Way of thinking and working.

(*n*) What is more important to you : money or the work?

Value behind

- What is the priority of the candidate?
- If you find better salary will you leave this job?

(*o*) How do you resolve conflict in your team?

Value behind

- The leadership qualities.
- Team spirit and co-ordination.

(*p*) How do you get best from the people working under/ with you?

Value behind

- Management skill.
- Way of dealing with people.

(*q*) What makes you different from others?

Value behind

- Your achievements.
- Your talents.

(*r*) What do you dislike most at work?

Value behind

- Your liking and disliking.
- If you like the job assigned to you.

(*s*) Would you mind if we take reference from your present/ past employer?

Value behind

- How do you react?
- If your present employer knows about your job search or not?

(*t*) Can you work under stress/pressure?

Value behind

- Your ability to handle the pressure.
- How you react with the situation?

(*u*) What qualities a manager should have?

Value behind

- Your managing skills.
- Style of functioning, coping with team.

(*v*) Are you satisfied with your present job?

Value behind

- Expectations regarding job.
- Priorities while choosing a job.
- Satisfaction and dissatisfaction in career.

(*x*) How long would you give your contribution to this company?

Value behind

- If you are sincere or not?
- Are you a static and realistic person?
- Your feelings about company.

(*y*) Where do you think to make improvements in yourself?

Value behind

- Your weakness and strength.
- Whether your weakness affects your performance or not.
- Your improving/learning capacity.

(*z*) How do you rate me as an interviewer?

Value behind

- Your opinion about him.
- Your comfortness and satisfaction to take a decision.

(*aa*) Do you have any question? or

You may ask any question to us.

Value behind

- Your eagerness and enthusiasm about job and company.
- To make sure that if they offer you the job, what decision would you take?

There are many more behavioural questions, which have sole aim to judge the keenness and ability to achieve excellence, through hard work, team spirit, dedication to the company, motivational approach and self-initiative of a candidate.

The candidate may ask some questions regarding job's responsibilities, such as:

(*a*) What is the strategy of the company regarding achievements?

(*b*) When would I know the outcome of this interview?

(*c*) Would you please explain me the organisational structure of the company?

(*d*) Would you please explain me the managerial philosophy of the company?

(*e*) How will my performance be evaluated?

(*f*) How many people have held this job in the last five years? On what position they are now?

(*g*) Would you tell me about the most successful people within the organisation?

(*h*) What are the three most important priorities for this position, to achieve in the first six months, and how would they be evaluated?

(*i*) What are the greatest strengths and the weakness of the department I am to handle?

(*j*) What will be the scope of my authority in running the departments?

When a candidate asks these thoughtful questions, positive attitude and enthusiasm reflect and prove his/her potential and uniqueness.

Right Approach

The right approach to the interview is to have a balanced view of the exercise. It is commonly seen that there are two extreme views among the candidates about the interview—

(*i*) Candidate deems interview something too enough and scaring. This automatically leads the candidates to a state of indifference and even diffidence and even a lack of desire for preparedness. Or contrarily, it makes them over-enthusiastic or unduly nervous, in which state thinking, planning, analysing or even answering are very difficult.

(*ii*) Candidates take interview as a cakewalk, a state in which they don't feel it necessary to have any prior preparations or plannings.

The right approach to the interview is a balanced, non-impassioned approach based on reason and with a clear understanding and realisation of the paramountcy of interview which can make or mar a candidate's career.

Overall, above all these necessities, success in interview can be positively and readily ensured by clearly understanding technique which includes its nature, scope, methodology, application and essentials.

The second impression is made during the interaction with interviewers with the help of all the above mentioned qualities.

○○○

Chapter 5

During the interview

> *When a candidate enters the interview room gently and greets all the members with a gentle smile and is asked to take the seat.*

What to do

- Must say thank you Sir/Ma'm.
- Sit attentively in a cool and collected manner.
- Handle your documents/file like a treasure.
- With soft smile look the main person in eyes.
- Appear comfortable, confident and interested.
- Listen carefully to interviewers.
- Convey your answer concisely in full sentences.
- Give authentic information regarding any details.
- Bend forward slightly while answering.
- Keep pleasant facial expression.
- Keep hands relaxed in the lap.
- Use hands to animate or express interest.
- Keep the voice tone audible, well modulated and relaxed.
- Be positive and confident.
- Be aware of mannerisms and show welcome mood for any question.
- Keep a balance between what you actually are and what you want to be.
- If you are complemented for the answers, remember to thank the interviewer.
- If your answer or opinions are rejected, remember to say sorry.

- Respond to the questions and support your answers about yourself with specific examples, whenever possible.

- Relate your answer to the point.

- Ask for clarification if you don't understand a question.

- Take the interview seriously, even if you might not be interested to join the company for some reason.

- As an interview is a two-way conversation, conduct yourself congenially and respectfully.

- Ask good and intelligent questions to the interviewer to get any information.

- Make sure about the next step in the selection process, try to know when and to whom you have to contact further.

- When the interview is concluded, convey your sincere thanks to all the members.

- Exhibit confidence and a positive attitude.

- Depart gracefully and not in a hurried manner.

- After the interview, make notes right away so that you can remember your mistakes during this interview.

- Write a thank you letter to your interviewer promptly.

- As per your subject and your job profile, try to give appropriate answers.

What not to do

- Don't appear too nervous or overconfident.

- Don't slouch or lean forward too much.

- Don't forget to say thanks for offering you the chair.

- Don't boast, people in front of you are wise enough to see through you.

- Don't scratch nose or arrange hair during the interview.

- Don't carry a key bunch or a pen in hands.

- Don't maintain or give any false information.

- Don't give additional information unless asked for.
- Never speak ill of your present/past/previous employer, colleague or boss.
- Don't give humorous or ironical answer.
- Don't obstruct the interviewer when he asks something.
- Don't repeat questions, answers, phrases or words.
- Never assign the reason for change saying regarding bad boss, poor salary, higher responsibilities, locations or poor chances of progress.
- Don't be in a hurry to complete the interview.
- Don't show your interest in the organisation because of its geographic location only.
- Don't show your eagerness for the job, even if you have more urgency.
- Don't show casualness or arrogance at the interview.
- Don't discuss about salary or perks unless some positive indication is given or asked by the interviewer.
- Don't argue with the interviewers on any matter or point.
- Don't try to influence the interviewers with your personal problems to gain sympathy.
- Don't take a cell phone call while at an interview. Keep it on vibration or just switch off.
- Don't forget to convey sincere thanks to the interviewer while you are leaving the interview hall.
- Don't forget to write a follow-up letter (thanks-giving letter) to the interviewer.

○○○

Chapter 6

Types of Interview

Each and every organisation has its own interview and selection process, which varies on the level, position and nature of job. Generally, for government job, preliminary and subjective main written test exams are held and those pass with high ranks are called for interview. In corporate sector job CVs or resumes or bio-datas of appropriate candidates are shortlisted and called for interview. The HR persons carry out a preliminary interview to check out the prima-facie suitability of the candidate. The candidates who get success in HR round, are called for technical round interview, where either the behavioural experts or senior persons may see the candidate to evaluate his/her suitability to the job and the organisation.

According to organisations and required job's nature of company, there may be the following types of interviews—

Preliminary Screening Interview

The main objective of this interview is to collect information and general description of the candidates to select the appropriate candidate for the required job and to weed out the ineligible applicants.

The representatives deputed by the companies screen the covering letters and the resumes of the applicants and ask questions to find out the inconsistencies mentioned and answers by them. They only find out whether the applicants fulfil the required parameters or not.

Sometimes this interview is taken through telephone or computer (internet) also.

To get success in this interview, mention only factual things which are written on resume. Get the notes and resume near by so that whatever questions are asked by the interviewer can be replied exactly and confidently.

The Stress Interview

In this materialistic and competitive world, sometimes every person feels stressed or tense. Stress is the result of interaction between individual and the environment in which one is working or leading life. The main purpose of the stress interview is to evaluate the ability of an individual to handle ambiguity and stress linked with the post such as the post of Personnel Manager, HR Manager, Industrial Relations Manager etc.

Stress interviews are a deliberate attempt to see how the candidate handles the demanding situations. The interviewer may be sarcastic or argumentative or may keep him waiting. The interviewer wants to know whether the candidate is irritated or disturbed or is able to solve the problem and handle the situation calmly. Interviewer see the stress interview as a legitimate way of determining candidates suitability for a position. As the employee goes up the ladder, the level of stress increases due to work-load and responsibilities.

Members of interview boards may fire questions one after other without reasonable interval. They can make some personal attack on the candidate regarding values and character. They may also use derogatory remarks by which the candidate can lose his/her mental balance.

The candidate should realise that he/she is facing stress interview, so they should respond the questions from the intellect rather than emotions, very calmly. Don't give explanation regarding poor performance or under-importance. At last forget all the things, because it was not personal.

Hands on Interview

In this type of interview, interviewer wants to see the candidate in action or solving practical problems with his/her knowledge and skills. For some jobs like computer programmers, engineers, accountants, marketing executives etc, this type of interview is taken. An engineer may be asked to do some analysis of an engineering problem; a marketing executive may be asked to analyse sales figures and a computer programmer may be asked to write a software programme.

A candidate should understand the given problem and requirement well, and then start taking action. With patience, one should demonstrate and find the solution of problem.

Lunch and Dinner Interview

This type of interview is usually held for the position which requires inter-personal acuity. It may be more casual, but the candidate should remember that it is a business lunch and he/she is being watched carefully. The interviewer wants to check the social etiquettes and the dealing power with a guest or business meeting as a host.

In this interview, the candidate should be relaxed with table manners. While ordering the meal, he/she should give all the priorities to the interviewer. Though the candidate is a guest here, he/she should try to play the role of a host. Always speak in low tone. Must say thanks after the meal.

Behavioural Interviews

This type of interview is held to judge and analyse the real attitude of the candidate. The sole aim of this interview is to judge the keenness and ability to achieve excellence, potential to succeed in an organisation through hard work, team spirit, motivational approach and self-initiative.

Through behavioural questions the interviewer wants to extract the hidden positive and negative qualities, strengths and weaknesses of the candidate. Some behavioural questions are:

- Why are you the best candidate for the job?
- What motivates you most?
- What is more important to you, financial success or job satisfaction?

- What's the value you'll bring to our organisation?
- How do you handle the pressure?
- What accomplishment are you most proud of?
- How do you deal with impossible deadlines?

While answering behavioural questions the candidate should always be polite and show the positive attitude. He/She should never pose his/herself as a person that never commits mistakes, as it is fact that none is perfect in this world. If possible, candidate should support the answers with demonstration or true stories and examples, because interviewer is interested to see some evidence to back up the answer given. The candidate should give straightforward explanation with clear objectives.

Structured and Unstructured Interviews

In a structured interview, the interviewer makes use of a previously compiled list of questions to identify the necessary skills, competencies, abilities and experience of the candidate, required for the job.

To handle structured interviews it is always good to gather information about the technical aspects of the job and study the relevant job description before the interview.

Unstructured interviews are used by the interviewer to make a delicate distinction between the candidates of the same qualities. Stress interviews are very good examples of the unstructured interviews. The aim of such interviews is to draw out a clear line amongst best candidates.

To handle this unstructured interview the candidate should focus on mental strengths and give priorities to the peoples' issue with cool and calm temperament.

Telephonic and Video Conferencing

Telephonic interviews are mainly taken to eliminate poorly qualified candidates. The candidate may be unaccustomed or inexperienced at dealing with conversations over the phone.

He/She might be called out of the blue or a telephone call to check on resume.

To handle the telephonic interview, the candidate should keep all the key information, including the resume, notes and cue cards next to the phone, so that he/she can give the answer clearly and soundly. The candidate should express interest in the job by closing with: "I am very interested in exploring my abilities with you. I am free either on such and such date, which if better for you, you can call me anyway." If the candidate gets a surprise call, he/she should ask to call back at a mutually agreeable time or offer to call back later by saying something like:

"I have a scheduling conflict at this time. Can I call you back tomorrow after working hours, if you have no problem or you may fix the time."

Now-a-days some employers have started using video-conferencing to conduct interviews. Conducting an interview via video-conferencing enables the employer to save time, expenses on travelling, but face-to-face interview is always effective.

To handle this interview the candidate should practise before a mirror and a video camera, so that he/she can face the camera and answer boldly as he/she is in front of the interviewer.

Walking Interview

It is an interview where a candidate is straight way invited through an advertisement, to appear direct for interview before an official of the company concerned at a particular place on a particular day and time. Now-a-days, walking interview is in general trend, because in much less time all the aspects of interview can be fulfilled by the organiser/companies. There is no unnecessary correspondence between the candidates and the organisation.

The filling up of application forms, submission of biodata etc are done just before or at the time of interview. The candidates' original testimonials are scrutinized then and there.

The candidate should check in the advertisement whether the job is suitable or not. If suitable, they should be ready with all the documents and testimonials, photos etc and with cool and calm mental status, reach at the venue half an hour before the interview time.

The aim of this interview is to check all the abilities of the candidate within a few minutes.

Personal or One-man Interview

In a small organisation, when vacant posts are in limited number, or when only a specialized person is required then one-man or personal interview is conducted. Though it may happen rarely yet it can happen that there is only one applicant for a post and if he/she fulfils all the necessary requirements and has the necessary experience as per his/her application then it is only a matter of satisfaction for the company to appoint him/her by ascertaining facts through a study of original testimonials etc, a single person can also handle that.

This interview is likely to be brief and less tiring both for the interviewer and the candidate. The candidate do not have to face different pulls and pushes which may sometime seem embarrasing to him/her. The company can save a lot of money by holding a one-man interview.

It is natural that every human being has some peculiar traits, tastes, aptitude and idiosyncracies. In this type of interview it is almost certain that the interview will select candidates according to the interviewer's taste only. The single interviewer can err in judgment and select a candidate who may prove a thorn in the company in the long run. In a nutshell, a one-man interview can cause losses to the company in the following way—wrong selection, favouritism, nepotism, casteism, agreement to extraordinary salary, perks, terms and conditions to a candidate.

For this interview, a candidate should try to realize that all the questions to be asked in all kinds of interviews are basically the same or of the some kind depending upon the nature of the job. The candidate should try to balance and talk in a friendly manner. If the interviewer seems to be strict, the candidate should be cautious and talk to him/her as he/she wants. The candidate should place all the relevant facts as demanded by the interviewer and try to substantiate them with documentary proof.

Panel Interview

In the panel interview because of the multiplicity of the number of interviewers, there is better possibility of fair play and impartiality than in the one-person interview. In this interview different members not only ask different questions but also talk about job requirements, terms and conditions, position and status of the company from different angles etc. In this way the candidate can get much more necessary information than in a one-man-interview which can sometimes prove like a closed fist, if the interviewer is too reserved or highbrow by nature for the candidate to present his own view-point not only regarding various topics but also his own terms.

Most of the big organisations like the Union Public Service Commission, Central Recruitment, Staff Selection Commission, State Bank Group, State Public Service Commission and several other boards and agencies conduct panel interviews where a very large number of candidates are taken and overall personality of the candidate is gauzed by the interview members.

In this interview a candidate should try to understand the psychology of each member, and answer the question in conformity and should behave as usual in a quite normal and simple way.

Sequential Interview

Sequential interview means a series of interviews one after another. In this interview the same candidate is judged by different interviewers individually. Each interviewer may ask different type of questions and may form his/her own objective opinion irrespective of the opinion formed by other interviewers. It is more comprehensively a matter of fact interview where the scope for wayward behaviour either by the candidate or by the interviewer is very much limited. It is comparatively tough and deeply probing, sometimes even a meritorious interviewee can feel perplexed and disgusted.

The candidate should take the sequential interview in a routine manner, and should not feel irritated. If in one interview a candidate feels that he/she has not been able to express his/herself properly or has failed to ask certain questions or seek certain information regarding the company or the terms and conditions of appointment, he/she should get this lapse or lacunae made up in the next interview. The candidate should not feel disappointed if sequential interview takes a lot of time.

Second Interview

Some Organisation/company or employers collect more and more resume of the candidates to find out more about the suitability of the candidate. Firstly, they shortlist the candidate after an initial screening interview and then conduct a second interview. It is aimed to ascertain that the first interview made an accurate assessment of the candidate. It's questions are generally aimed to analyse about the candidate's capacity and approach towards work. Sometimes candidates are asked to perform some work, to evaluate the ability of candidate's to handle the given responsibility. The interviewers like to be assured about any doubt, during the prior interview.

Final Interview

After getting success in the previous stages of selection, sometimes final interview is conducted by the employer though it is a formality. Often the CEO or the head of the company attends the interview either alone or with one or two other executives. This is the final stage of selection where some formal questions are asked by the Head/CEO/Chairman of the organisation to know each other.

Case Interview

A case interview is a job interview in which the applicant is given a question/situation/problem/challenge and asked to resolve that. The case problem is often a business situation or a business case that the interviewer has worked on in real life.

After the applicant is given information about the case, he is expected to ask the interviewer logical and sequential questions that will enable him to understand the situation, probe deeper into relevant areas, gather pertinent information and arrive at a solution or recommendation for the question or situation at hand.

Case interviews are mostly used in hiring for management consulting and investment banking jobs. Firms use case interviews to evaluate analytical ability and problem-solving skills; they are looking not for a "correct" answer but for an understanding of how the applicant thinks and how he approaches problems.

During case interviews, interviewers are generally looking for the following skills:

- Numerical and Verbal Reasoning Skills
- Communication and Presentation Skills
- Business Skills and Commercial Awareness

Candidates are often asked to estimate a specific number, often a commercial figure (such as market size or profitability). Candidates are expected to demonstrate reasoning rather than producing the exact answer.

A case interview can also be conducted as a group exercise. Here, several candidates are given some briefing materials on a business problem and asked to discuss and agree upon a solution. The interviewers normally sit around the exterior of the room as silent observers. They assess candidates' communication and interaction as well as analytical thinking and commercial awareness.

Ladder Interview

A ladder interview is an interviewing technique where a seemingly simple response to a question is pushed by the interviewer in order to find subconscious motives.

Example

It begins with a simple question, and then another question is asked about that response. For example, an interviewer may ask: "How come you skipped class?" and the response may be: "I went out with my friends". The next question would be something like "Why did you go out with your friends?" Essentially, the format is as follows:

Interviewer: "Why x?"
Subject: "Because z"
Interviewer: "Why z?"
Subject: "Because b"
Interviewer: "Why b?"

The first responses are generally functional justifications, like "I went out with my friends because I wanted some pizza", or "I wanted some pizza because I used to eat it as a child"; but eventually the interviewer hopes to reach a virtue justification like "It's good to be childish". Then it is fair to conclude that the interviewee skipped class because he valued childishness.

Usage

This technique is used for marketing in order to see what values inspire the consumption of the particular product. A chocolate bar producer would do this test so they can match the most common terminal virtue to their product in an advertisement. For example, the virtue of justice, or a virtue of efficiency, or in the above example, the virtue of childhood.

Campus Interview

Campus placement or campus interview is the program conducted within the educational institutes or in a common place to provide job to the students pursing or in the stage of completing the programme. In this program industries will visit the college to select the qualified students.

Types of campus placement

There are two types of campus placement.

They are: on campus and off campus

On campus placement

This is the placement program organized only for the students within the educational institute. In most cases students in the final year of a program will participate in this placement program.

Off campus placement

This job placement program is for students from other institutions. This program will be conducted in a common place (it may be in a college or in some public place) where students from different colleges will take part.

Project Placement

Companies recruit students to do their academic project in the industrial environment.

Student Internship Placement

Companies recruit the students as interns. Internship will be during their student period.

Objective

The major objective of campus placement is to identify the talented and qualified professionals during their persual of an educational program. This process reduces the time for an industry to pick the candidates according to their needs.

Procedure

There are few factors that affect a student before he appears for the campus placement. They are:

Pre-placement Talk

A presentation about the company will be made during the pre-placement talk. Basically, the presentation includes the information like selection procedure, company's milestones, organizational achievements, candidate scope of improvement within the organization if selected, salary, employment benefits. Usually this presentation ends up with question and answer session, students are given chance to ask questions about company.

Educational Qualification

Companies who are interested in campus visit for recruitment purpose will have specific qualification criteria. Qualification criteria include marks or grade range, specific programme, etc.

Written Test

Qualified students will undergo a test. This is usually a simple aptitude test but depending on company the difficulty level of the test may be at the higher side.

Group Discussion

Most of the companies will have this round as a clearing and or filtering round. This round may or may not be conducted; depending upon the company this round may be included in the selection process.

A common topic is placed before the group and a formal discussion or knowledge sharing is expected by the judge. Purpose of this round is to check communication skills, etiquette of person, listening ability, convincing power, group leadership, leader or follower and many other things are evaluated on the basis of requirement or the particular intention of organisation or company.

Lecturettes

Lecturette is a short lecture. It is a sort of short speech test, imparting knowledge and passing information. Companies lay emphasis on the power of speech. It is a means through which a candidate can impress interviewers by his expression, fluency, manners, elasticity of thoughts and delivery.

Remember. "Spoken words rule the world".

In lecuretters, the interviewer gives each candidate a card on which 3 or 4 topics are printed relating to current-affairs, political events or topics on social, economic environment and technology. Each candidate is called by turn to pick up a card. He is asked to select anyone of the topics given therein. He is then allowed to go a little away from the group and prepare his speech or lecturette for about 3 minutes. Then he is asked to make a short speech not exceeding 3 to 5 minutes time. This is an extempore lecture whereby one can impress interviewers by his eloquency and delivery of speech. It is of great importance that a candidate should choose such a subject about which he has sufficient knowledge.

Technical Interview

Based on outcome of above said process, students will further undergo a round called technical round. This round evaluates the technical ability of the student. Most of the cases this will be an individual round or it may be grouped with the formal interview. Most important at 'technical interview' is mutuality (interviewee and interviewer) and sincerity.

Formal Interview

Final round of the selection process, where the student's stability and his confidence level towards the particular work will be evaluated.

Post-placement Talk

Once the student is selected, he will be given an offer letter. Company's executive may provide guidelines about joining procedure and other prerequisites if needed

○○○

Chapter 7

Model Interviews for Different Jobs

For Civil Services

UPSC comprise of All India Services like the Indian Administrative Service, Indian Foreign Service, Indian Police Service, Indian Forest Service and other like IA & IS, Customs, Income-tax and all the top class services in key positions of different branches of Administration.

Model Interview for Indian Administrative Service

Model Interview-1

Vishwanath Jatar, our first candidate for the interview, is of lean built, medium height and average complexion. His large brownish eyes reflect interest, friendliness and sincerity. He sports a light blue colour summer suit which fits him smartly with his average light complexion. It also makes him appear to be dressed formally for the occasion while at the same time allowing him to remain comfortable in the late-April warm weather of Delhi. His brisk and active movements indicate energy, enthusiasm and purposiveness. He walks with firm steps and measured strides, keeping himself erect and straight. His gait adds to his personality, displaying confidence and self-assurance. The warm and sincere smile playing on his lips and spontaneously reflected in his eyes indicates friendliness and cordiality. He looks cheerful, lively and affable. He arrives well on time at the UPSC premises in an auto and completes the preliminaries like filling up of forms, production of original certificates, etc.

The Interview

Jatar: (*Standing to attention*) Good morning to you all, Sirs.

Chairman: Good morning, Mr. Jatar. Please be seated.

Jatar: Thank you, Sir. (*He occupies the chair indicated without any noise or unnecessary movements. While seated with poise, he remains relaxed but attentive to the Board.*)

Chairman: From your dossier, I see you have done Maths, Physics and Chemistry in your Higher Secondary and B.Sc. (Hons.). But for M.A. you have opted for Economics. As for the IAS, I find one of your optional is History. (*Smiling*) Why such changes? Do you wish to be a jack of all trades?

Jatar: (*Reciprocating the smile*). You are right, Sir and I agree that the changes in the subjects of my study may seem odd. But they were dictated by the circumstances and adopted to suit certain objectives. Originally, my aim was to do engineering, but in the entrance exams after plus two stage, I could not make it to the merit list. Neither could I afford the huge capitation fees to join engineering independently. I decided to continue with the same subjects in the college so that I could try for engineering even as an Hons. graduate. Another reason is that I was familiar with the subjects and could score higher marks as compared to humanities. Higher marks help to get into MBA, Civil Services and similar competitive exams. I also appeared for the IIM Entrance Examination, but did not make it to that also. At this stage, I decided to concentrate on IAS. Since Economics is helpful for business as well as for IAS, I opted for it for my M.A. in preference to Maths. I chose History as one of the optional for Civil Services Exam, as I found the subject interesting besides helping me to score higher marks. You see, Sir, I have adapted myself to achieving my objective.

Chairman: Will you not feel disappointed with the IAS when you first wanted to be an engineer?

Jatar: Certainly not, Sir. As I mentioned I can adjust and adapt myself. Besides, I would have opted for the IAS, even as an engineer. The IAS is now open for technocrats and their inclusion will enrich the cadre in the context of our efforts to revitalise public sector with emphasis on higher technology. I have opted for the IAS consciously with the conviction that I would get full job satisfaction and that I could make meaningful contribution to the job.

1st Member: According to the critics, the IAS has now become the puppet of the politicians who are accused of interfering too much in the functioning of IAS officials. How would you cope with this problem?

Jatar: In a parliamentary democracy like ours, the politicians voted to power are accountable to the legislature and electorate and thus carry higher responsibilities. At the same time, an efficient Civil Service is indispensable for parliamentary democracy to provide good administration as also to provide continuity and stability. However, we are also aware of growing day-to-day interference by politicians in the functioning of IAS officials. While this is not desirable, there are, to my mind, two main reasons for this interference. Firstly, a large number of politicians are not educated to the required standard to appreciate the actions taken by an IAS Officer. Instead, motivated by the vote bank politics, they rush in as saviour of masses even in cases where decisions are taken as per rules and regulations. And secondly, even the electorate are to blame. They want their representatives to get things done in their favour even if rules do not permit so. If the politician does not oblige them, he earns their ire and fearing that his prospects for re-election may be jeopardised, he succumbs to their pressure and interferes. Thirdly, the notion spread in post-independence period that bureaucrats are public servants meant to cater to whims of the masses, right or wrong, has wrongly been interpreted and hence misused.

However, I will not be a servile or sycophant IAS Officer, but act as an impartial, upright and rules-respecting officer without worrying for plum postings or loaves or fishes of office.

2nd Member: But amidst rampant corruption and by and large, a subservient Civil Service, do you think you alone can clean the Augean stables?

Jatar: Why not Sir. I will not be alone in this crusade. You must be aware, Sir, that there is already a strong move among IAS Officers to expose the corrupt among themselves. I will join the band of such dedicated and clean officers who would administer as per Rule Book without succumbing to the unreasonable pressure or interference of politicians. At the same time, I will see to it that no injustice is done to the man 'without connection'.

2nd Member: What would be your alternative choice if you do not make the grade in the Civil Services?

Jatar: I shall try again and again with redoubled effort to make certain that I prove successful. I am confident that I will surely make it to the IAS. However, for argument's sake, assuming that I had to seek some other career, my preference would be to start a medium or small scale industry of my own.

2nd Member: To launch an industry you need adequate finance. I heard you saying that you could not afford the huge capitation fee for engineering admission. Besides, one also requires knowledge and experience to run an industry. How would you overcome these obstacles?

Jatar: I have some affluent friends who are keen to start some industrial ventures as sleeping partners. I can start the project as a joint venture with them. Even if this does not materialise, I can take loan from a bank to start a small scale industry. The Government has been liberally giving loans to the unemployed graduates and youth. However, before launching the industry, I shall make it a point to get all the knowledge required for it, and for this, I would work as an apprentice for a year or so to one of my maternal uncles who has a flourishing small scale industry in steel furniture. With this experience and backing of my uncle who would, I am sure, pass on some of his surplus orders to me. I am confident, I would succeed since where there is a will, the way can be found out.

1st Member: Which is a better career in your opinion— the Civil Services, Armed Forces or the private enterprises?

Jatar: As I submitted earlier Sir, my preference is for the IAS and I regard it best so far as my background, aptitude and choice are concerned. In general, each profession has its own distinct merits and the choice depends on the individual and his qualifications and aptitude. In my view, as an IAS Officer, one has wider linkage with masses and classes, wider power and prestige than other services.

3rd Member: What effect did global economic crisis have on Asia, according to the United Nations and Asian Development Bank report?

Jatar: The global economic crisis has upset the pace of Asia's development as far as its poverty eradication is concerned. It is said to have driven 21 million more people in the region into poverty. As per a joint report by the UN and the Asian Development Bank, the global economic slowdown has slowed down trade, affected export very badly as well as slashed tourism receipts and pushed up unemployment rate. All these have resulted in a state where it has become very difficult for the region to achieve its Millennium Development Goals. These goals range from halving extreme poverty to curbing the spread of HIV and AIDS and providing universal primary education. The region had set the target date of 2015.

3rd Member: Can you say something about the notable gains the region posted prior to recent global meltdown?

Jatar: Before the global meltdown, the region, on the whole, posted significant gains in its Millennium Development Goals commitments and was on track to achieve three important targets that included gender parity in secondary education, ensuring access of children to primary schools and halving the proportion of people living below poverty line or in extreme poverty.

3rd Member: What does the term "new poor" refer to?

Jatar: The term "new poor" is actually used to identify those people who were rendered jobless after the global meltdown. According to the International Labour Organisation, the number of unemployed people in Asia has gone up to 98 million in 20.... This raised the unemployment level from 4.7 per cent in 20...

to 5.1 per cent in 20.... Job losses coupled with inadequate social protection has forced more people into poverty.

3rd Member: What should be the way out, according to you, for a faster growth?

Jatar: The report itself has hinted at the measures to overcome the problem. According to it, if fiscal stimulus packages have a strong component of social expenditures, this is likely to produce a double dividend—faster economic growth and accelerating progress towards Millennium Development Goals. I am also of the same view. Most stimulus packages have so far not paid serious attention to areas of social expenditures.

4th Member: Some experts think that successful Indo-Pakistan dialogue can lead to peace and prosperity. Do you think so?

Jatar: I subscribe to their view. But it does not seem, I mean Indo-Pak dialogue's success, possible owing to the communal views today in both the countries. Such an epic event cannot be possible simply by the leaders meeting and talking. It has to have powerful awakening among the masses on both sides of the border. At that, the Kashmir has become a perennial bone of contention. The Kashmir dispute has assumed both communal and military nature. Leave alone Kashmir, China and the United States tacitly support Pakistan, which prevents Pakistan settling for a positive solution.

4th Member: What do you mean by awakening among the masses? Do you want to say that political establishments of the two countries cannot solve the problem?

Jatar: Yes Sir, that is what I want to suggest. The army can win only with the common people endorsing the action. If peace has to be achieved, there must be a people's peace movement. What we need today is people's peace. The Indian and Pakistani people will show their patriotism only when they stop the confrontation between their countries. A creative federalism can put an end to war. An atmosphere of mutual harmony and understanding can be thought of only if both politicians and people on both sides are determined to end the existing animosity. Nevertheless, Pakistan has to accept Kashmir as an integral part of India as the pre-condition for Indo-Pakistan rapport. Everyone in Pakistan knows that the Maharaja made that State an integral part of the Indian Republic through a legal accession. We have to realise the fact that any religion which divides becomes irreligious.

5th Member: What is your opinion about the Protection of Women from the Domestic Violence Act?

Jatar: Sir, this Act came into effect in October 2006 with an objective of providing for more effective protection of the rights of women guaranteed under the Constitution, who are victims of violence of any kind occurring within the family. The Act provides for an inbuilt mechanism to facilitate the entire system of access to justice. But we know, a crucial step towards ensuring the success of any law is monitoring its implementation.

5th Member: Was this Act implemented across the country?

Jatar: Though this Act was implemented throughout the country, looking at the available data, we observed that the implementation of the Act was not uniform across the country. In most States, the protection officers were appointed at the district level, whereas in some States like Rajasthan, Punjab and Haryana, no protection officers were appointed. In these States, aggrieved persons had to rely on the police. There were some other factors also responsible for varying degrees of implementation and non-implementation.

Chairman: All seem to agree that lack of education and still prevailing high rate of illiteracy is the stumbling block towards our unity and progress. What do you think is the best way to overcome this problem in the shortest possible time?

Jatar: The Navodaya Schools, Sainik Schools and Kendriya Vidyalayas are the best answer to the school-going children. We must extend their reach all over India, covering all our villages and towns and cities. Central universities and open universities are the answer for higher learning. TV, Video, Radio, Internet, Cinema and other modern aids should be fully mobilised for spreading literacy, particularly adult education.

> ***Final Comments:*** *A brilliant and capable candidate who is endowed with all-round distinction and leadership ability. He displays excellent grasp in understanding complex problems with their short-term as well as long-term implications. His bold and pragmatic approach coupled with enthusiasm and optimism enable him to face new challenges with success.*

Model Interview-2

The second candidate, Yogesh Chandra Bhasin, a first divisioner in M.A. (Political Science) from Delhi University, is a dynamic young man of average height and medium build. His height can be reckoned around 172 cms., but he appears rather tall thanks to the high-heeled shoes he is sporting. Keeping the Delhi summer in mind, he has opted for light-grey pants and cream shirt which fit him well and also meet the requirements of the formal occasion. His shining black shoes and dark blue socks match admirably with his outfit and make him appear smart and efficient. He has kept his wavy, dark, well-grown hair slightly long, but it is properly shampooed and combed after a recent hair-cut. His personal hygiene is well-attended to and the thin moustache he sports adds to his impressive appearance. Overall, he is successful in creating a first favourable impression by his careful grooming, choice of well-fitting dress and upright carriage. He walks with confident steps, head held high and chest forward displaying self-confidence and resoluteness. By looking at him, one cannot but conclude that he is serious about the interview and keen to do well as he has taken the trouble to dress and present himself in the right manner before the Interview Board.

The Interview

Chairman: Good morning Mr. Bhasin, please take your seat and make yourself comfortable. If you require anything in particular, please do not hesitate to ask and we shall do our best to meet your needs.

Bhasin: Thank you Sir, and good morning to you all. (*He occupies the chair meant for the candidate smartly*). I am comfortable and ready, Sir and I do not need anything more. Thank you once again, Sir.

Chairman: Mr. Bhasin, I find from your dossier that you have studied Political Science at the University and gained first division M.A. in the subject. Does it show your intention to become a politician and enter active politics?

Bhasin: (Smiling) No Sir, not at all. Neither then, nor now, I am keen on becoming a politician. My goal has always been the IAS and I chose Political Science as one of my subjects of academic study, as I felt it would help me to discharge my responsibilities effectively as an administrator.

Chairman: That is interesting. Can you explain how the study of Political Science can be helpful to an IAS officer?

Bhasin: Sir, after Independence, India has opted for a democratic form of government with Parliamentary institutions fashioned on the British Westminster model. Our Constitution guarantees certain Fundamental Rights to its citizens. It also contains a chapter on Directive Principles indicating the direction or objectives towards which the nation should make progress. We have a welfare state founded on democratic socialism. Five-Year Plans have been formulated as the vehicles to enable the citizens to reap the benefits of this welfare state. The administrator has to play a key role in implementing the Five Year Plans and other related programmes in the context of the welfare state, socialism, democracy, fundamental rights of the citizens, parliamentary form of government responsible to the people, hopes and aspirations of the people and similar other factors. By studying Political Science, not only we can understand the working of our own Constitution and institutions but also know how they work in other democracies. Thus, I am convinced that the study of Political Science could be of great help to the administrators.

Chairman: Well, I agree you have something there, although many, who have not studied Political Science, have also become excellent administrators, both in India and abroad. But tell me why you do not want to join active politics. Is it your view that educated youth should eschew active politics?

Bhasin: No Sir, not at all. I wonder whether I had conveyed such an impression, if so, I am very sorry indeed. I firmly believe that good education is the basic and fundamental requirement to all, no matter one's profession or vocation in life. It is all the more so in the case of politicians. Of course, it will also help if politicians undergo the study of Political Science as an academic subject.

Chairman: Then why are you not keen on joining active politics?

Bhasin: (*Smiling*) Shall I say Sir that it calls for certain type of mental attitude, adjustability and adaptability to function as a successful politician. Secondly, you must have a special interest and drive for active politics. Above all, politics is an expensive game and you need a lot of money. May be I lack these and in any case, as I said earlier, my goal right from the beginning has been to join the IAS and I deliberately did not allow myself to be led away from my chosen goal.

1st Member: I suppose you are aware that the world, which, of course, includes our country also, has seen many able politicians who did not have any formal university education. For example, one can cite some well known film-star politicians.

Bhasin: I beg your pardon, Sir. I referred to good education, if I remember correctly and not to formal university education and acquisition of degrees as such. The great Winston Churchill and Abraham Lincoln did not boast of Master's degrees. But they, by their own efforts, acquired good education. The film-star politicians, I would say, are exceptions to the rule. Even they could shine as still better politicians, if they had university education. I would cite the example of N. T. Ramarao in Andhra Pradesh, MGR and Jayalalitha in Tamil Nadu and Vinod Khanna and Shatrughan Sinha at the Centre under the previous NDA Government as also President Reagan of the USA who, equipped with good education, have delivered goods quite creditably.

1st Member: You indirectly referred to money power in politics. Can you say that we have been successful in operating democracy in independent India and that it has taken roots in this country?

Bhasin: All I can say is that we are still retaining democracy in this land even after 7 decades of Independence and in the face of many diversities, whereas it has fallen by the wayside in most other countries which opted for democracy on attaining Independence after World War II. That is an achievement in itself. As for its taking roots here, I have my own doubts. I am inclined to agree with Dr. Ambedkar who observed that democracy in India is nothing but top dressing on alien soil. To strike deep roots, democracy has to grow through evolution with people getting used to it. They must have education and acquire a stake in preserving democratic institutions. A citizen should know the value of his vote and exercise it judiciously and with care and caution. All these are absent in our country. In India, money and muscle power, caste consideration and gender play a dominant role. There are only a few top leaders who are elected on the basis of merit.

2nd Member: You have indicated Haryana as your home State, but have received all your college and university education in Delhi. How do you explain this?

Bhasin: My great-grandfather migrated from West Punjab (Pakistan). We are now settled down in Gurgaon where my father and elder brother are running a small factory producing various automobile components. Though in Haryana, Gurgaon is just an hour's bus journey from Delhi which is hub of academic activities providing state-of-the art educational facilities. Hence, I chose Delhi for higher studies.

2nd Member: What have you been doing since completing your M.A. studies?

Bhasin: Mainly, I have been preparing for the IAS. Occasionally, I have been helping my father in the marketing of the automobile components.

2nd Member: Why marketing and not production?

Bhasin: (Smiles) Well Sir, anyone with some financial resources can produce anything. But marketing and selling and realisation of sales revenue are quite different and the most difficult areas. Besides, I am not an engineer or technician. Above all, marketing provides good scope for travelling which I enjoy.

2nd Member: If you are selected for the lAS, which State cadre would you like to opt and why?

Bhasin: I would like to go to either Nagaland, Mizoram or Arunachal Pradesh. In my view, these are some States which pose very challenging tasks for an administrator.

3rd Member: How do you interpret the IMF forecasts in regard to global economic affairs?

Bhasin: Sir, my view about the International Monetary Fund (IMF) forecasts does not differ from the common perception. It is said to be more authentic and accurate than the World Bank and other international institutions. For instance, I am convinced of its forecasting in the latest World Economic Outlook that the world economy will recover from the economic crisis faster than previously thought. As per its forecast, world output is thought to be growing at 4.2 per cent in 20.... It had earlier, in the January 20... projection, put the growth rate at 3.9 per cent. According to the IMF, advanced economies, including the US and the Euro Zone countries, are set to grow by 2.2 per cent in 20.... Like that of the previous year, the ongoing recovery will continue to be uneven. The US is off to a better start than Europe and Japan, according to its forecast.

3rd Member: What about China and India, if you talk of Japan?

Bhasin: Sir, emerging Asian economies led by China and India are in the forefront of the recovery, according to the IMF. In comparison, many countries in the Commonwealth of Independent States are lagging behind. China and India have been said to grow by 10 per cent and 8.8 per cent, respectively in 20.... It is worth noting that the forecast for India has been raised by a considerable 1.1 percent, whereas the one for China remains the same as it was in January 20....

The IMF has found the Indian economy more resilient than it was thought earlier. It has taken into account the series of recent upbeat economic news to base its forecast. What is interesting is that the IMF's projected growth rate for India is much higher than what the RBI has forecast i.e. 8 per cent for 20...-20....

3rd Member: Has the IMF suggested anything to achieve the global recovery?

Bhasin: Yes Sir, it has. According to it, global recovery is still fragile and the fiscal stimulus planned for 20... should be implemented. As it thinks, a policy agenda for achieving strong, sustained and balanced growth could require including other things, fiscal consolidation in advanced countries, exchange rate adjustments and a rebalancing of demand the world over.

4th Member: Can you throw some light on the reported continued infighting between the Palestinian groups, the Fatah and the Hamas?

Bhasin: Yes Sir, I can. This continued infighting between these two main Palestinian groups would lead to disaster. By disaster I mean that it would give a blow to the hope of a solution to the six-decade-old conflict with Israel as the situation is going to worsen day by day owing to the infighting. The infighting started some years ago and since June 20..., the energy and attention of these Palestinian groups have been consumed by infighting. Besides, people living in the West Bank and Gaza have got frustrated and have been expressing their resentment. What is the most disappointing outcome of this infighting is that it has fuelled extreme, al-Qaeda inspired Islamist groups which had hitherto been non-existent with regard to the Palestinian resistance.

4th Member: How have al-Qaeda inspired Islamist groups affected the course of the Palestinian resistance?

Bhasin: Some time back, the al-Qaeda inspired groups reportedly carried out provocative rocket attacks on Israel, whereas for a year or so, the Hamas had desisted from firing rockets into Israel. In a sense it was an unofficial ceasefire. But Israel did not go into the heart of the matter and held the Hamas responsible for these attacks. Israel retaliated by sending in troops and tanks into the Gaza strip and destroying houses there.

4th Member: What did the Hamas do to clear its actual stand?

Bhasin: The Hamas has attempted to rein in these alQaeda groups, broadly called Jihadi Salafis. Some of the Salafis were arrested too. In the Hamas-led raids many Salafis died too. In August 20..., one of the Salafi groups, Jund Ansar Allah, had challenged the Hamas in a Gaza mosque. The Jund Ansar Allah chief, Abdul Latif Musa had even declared Gaza to be an Islamic state. He had proclaimed his group's intention to carry on violent resistance against Israelis. Besides, he had even dared the Hamas to act against it. As the Hamas was left with no option, it retaliated and killed all the 27 members of the group, including its leader.

4th Member: How do you distinguish between the Fatah and the Hamas?

Bhasin: The Hamas refuses to recognise Israel, whereas the Fatah has long recognised Israel and has been comfortable talking to it.

5th Member: What is your opinion regarding the recent China-Pakistan nuclear deal?

Bhasin: It does not bode well for India. The Indian concern over this deal is very genuine, because Pakistan has an established track record of proliferation. This deal has to have some global response too and might trigger some debate in the international-community. That is why, the Chinese officials continued to deny that any such deal was in place till very recently. When the news had already become public and it was impossible to deny, an official only said curtly that while the Chinese government had given its backing to the deal in principle, some final details still had to be ironed out.

5th Member: What type of deal it is and has it followed the International Atomic Energy Agency (IAEA) norms?

Bhasin: No, the Chinese officials did not say anything about the IAEA norms. China's biggest operator of nuclear power plants, the China National Nuclear Corporation confirmed that it would export two 340 MW nuclear power reactors to Pakistan in a $2.375-billion agreement, in a controversial deal that analysts said, went against the internationally-mandated guidelines governing the transfer of nuclear technology.

5th Member: How do you think this deal went against internationally mandated guidelines?

Bhasin: To my mind, this deal went against internationally mandated guidelines, because the Chinese officials kept mum over the question whether China had approached the Nuclear Suppliers Group (NSG) or how it planned to secure a waiver. China has been a member of NSG since 2004. The NSG does not allow the sale of nuclear equipment to countries that have not signed the Nuclear Non-Proliferation Treaty and do not have a Comprehensive Safeguards Agreement with the IAEA. That is why, when India had signed the civilian nuclear agreement with the United States, this requirement was waived. The Chinese officials fervently defended China's nuclear relationship with Pakistan, amid concerns over Pakistan's proliferation record which is common knowledge now. It is the same China which had voiced opposition to the India-US civil nuclear deal. According to China, possible concerns in India regarding the deal would not be relevant to China's nuclear engagement with Pakistan.

> ***Comments:*** *The candidate shows excellent understanding of current national and international events and trends. He is aware of latest developments in this field and there is sound logic and reasoning in his arguments.*

Model Interview-3

The third candidate, Pankaj Kumar Verma is a round faced, fairly tall, fair-complexioned young man of lean and athletic build. He has a pleasant countenance with a friendly smile, which at once makes him endearing to others. His dark as well as large and lively eyes reflect warmth, sincerity and interest. From his dress and grooming one can readily infer that the candidate is serious about the interview and has taken good care to present himself in favourable light at the interview. He arrives at the UPSC building for this IFS interview along with another candidate, Mr. Tiwari, on his motorcycle about an hour earlier, which gives him ample time to fill in the forms, complete the preliminaries, study the seating plan and interview roster for the day and orient himself well to the surroundings.

The Interview

Chairman: Mr. Verma, from your bio-data, I find that you are now working as a sales executive in a firm which markets sports gears. Why did you select this job? Are you keenly interested in sports?

Verma: *(Smiling pleasantly)* To be frank, Sir, I have no claims for distinction in sports though I am interested in sports activities and played for my college various games like cricket, football and hockey. The job of the sales executive offers me good scope for travelling, seeing new places and getting to know more people. Hence, I opted for this in preference to the offer of lectureship in a tutorial college and front office assistant or receptionist in a five-star hotel.

Chairman: Since your goal is the IAS, I would have thought the lecturer's job would have been a better choice. It would have kept you in touch with your studies or the five-star hotel assignment could be more exciting since they pay very high salaries and perks in the hotel industry.

Verma : You are right, Sir. There is merit in what you have pointed out. However, I looked at it from another angle. As I explained the sales executive assignment gave me the opportunity to travel. I belong to U.P. and I wanted to know first-hand experiences about the places and people of my State. My ambition is to join the U.P. cadre as an IAS officer and serve my people as a District Magistrate. Hence, the more I learn of the State through direct contact, the better it would be for me. Next, I also like to enlarge the circle of my friends. Lastly, I also got the opportunity to visit various other States, besides U.P. It was a very interesting and revealing experience. I could compare and contrast the progress of U.P. with other States.

First Member: How does U.P. compare with other States you have visited?

Verma: In terms of industrial growth, literacy, employment opportunities, modern amenities like water, roads, power, communication etc., States like Maharashtra, Tamil Nadu, Gujarat, Punjab and Haryana are better off than U.P. But the people in U.P., are peace-loving, and tensions and industrial unrest are less there. However, much needs to be done to improve the standards of living of the masses in U.P. My home State has the advantage of fertile land with perennial water sources. The important rivers like Ganga and Yamuna and their tributaries carry water round the year. With the application of modern science and technology, spread of literacy and cooperation of the people and the Government, we can do wonders.

First Member: But how is it that U.P. is listed among the BIMARU States along with Bihar, M.P. and Rajasthan?

Verma: The maladies which this State has been suffering include overpopulation, too much dependence on agriculture (78% population), unwieldy size, despite creation of Uttarakhand. Besides being the most populous State with a population of over 19.98 crore in 2011 (one-fifth of country's total population), with a density of 829 per sq. km as against all-India average of 382, Uttar Pradesh has a literacy rate of just 67.7% against all India average of 73.0% as per 2011 Census. In fact, Uttar Pradesh has three distinct divisions, the affluent Western UP, Central UP and most backward Eastern UP. Political stability has eluded the State since 1990 due to the social forces unleashed by implementation of Mandal Commission Report and Ayodhya Movement. Resultantly, planned development of the State has suffered. But now when there is a government with full majority installed in the state, we may expect planned development in UP. The affluent Western UP has always been managing a lion's share in development effort while the backward eastern UP continues to languish in poverty.

Second Member: There is a vociferous demand by the regional parties for greater State autonomy. Do you feel greater autonomy and powers to the States will lead to faster economic growth and development of the people?

Verma: *(Smiles)* According to theory, Sir, decentralisation of power and authority should help growth and development. But in the case of our country, we have to take an overall view. During the British days, Calcutta (now Kolkata), Bombay (now Mumbai) and Madras (now Chennai) Presidencies received direct and major attention. Hence, they registered good development. But others, particularly the princely States, remained feudal and backward. To ensure balanced development of all regions and States in India, we have to have a strong Centre with full powers over all the States and regions. Secondly, if we had two all-India political parties like the Democrats and Republicans in the USA, or the Conservatives and Labour in the UK, we could take the risk of giving greater autonomy to the States, while maintaining the strength at the Centre through the political parties. But the only all-India party we had till 1977 and thereafter in 1980-89 and 1991-96, was the Indian National Congress. Even the Congress of today seems to have lost its appeal in many States where local or regional parties have captured power.

Third Member: But to my mind even a coalition Government consisting of more than 20 political parties can survive at the Centre. Do you agree?

Verma: I agree Sir. But that Government has to make a lot of compromise on many issues that are detrimental to our national fabric. For example, the 24-party NDA Government headed by Mr. Atal Behari Vajpayee could survive its full tenure, catering to some of the demands-often unreasonable of its regional partners which always insisted on their "pound of flesh" in total disregard of national interest. One of its erstwhile coalition partners, DMK and its ally MDMK were supporters of LTTE. They are proven anti-Hindi and anti-North parties proclaiming to be original inhabitants of the country *i.e.,* the Dravidians. Again, after the demand for Khalistan in Punjab has been quelled, Jammu and Kashmir, North Eastern States pose a threat to national integrity through a large number of militant outfits, besides Naga outfits demanding secession from India. Hence, greater State autonomy at this juncture might harm national unity and integrity. Above all, we have serious external threats from Pakistan and China. Despite being a victim of 9/11, the USA is conniving at Pak-sponsored terrorism in Jammu and Kashmir and other parts of India for its overall national interests to fight the remnants of the Taliban in Afghanistan and to capture fugitive Osama bin Laden. Hence, I feel we should maintain a strong Centre at this point of time.

Fourth Member: What about Indian culture? It is said to be the unifying and cementing force. Will Indian culture not take care of unity?

Verma: I agree with you that Indian culture does have some unifying effect. But this is based on customs, traditions, philosophy and outlook. However, all these are related to the past and are undergoing significant changes in the context of our independence, contact with the West and exposure to modern education and mass media. Above all, Indian culture is caste oriented and hence divisive to that extent. For instance, if there had been mass resistance to the invaders and had they joined battle with their Kshatriya brothers, many invasions would not have taken place in India. Indian culture has undergone much changes with the onslaught of Western materialism. Hence, it may be unwise to rely solely on Indian culture to preserve the unity and integrity of the country.

Fourth Member: Do you not think that the pledge with regard to global strategic partnership between US and India will work out?

Verma: I do not mean that. The India-US Counter-terrorism Cooperation Initiative, explained by the joint statement of Mr. Barack Obama and Indian Prime Minister, is of course very significant. But the joint statement's content itself evidently addresses India's concern that the US was not condemnatory enough of Pakistan's perceived inability to rein in terrorism. The joint statement expressed strong concern about the threat posed by terrorism and violent extremists emanating from India's neighbourhood whose impact is felt beyond the region. That is why the two leaders agreed that resolute and credible steps must be taken to eliminate safe havens and sanctuaries that provide shelter to terrorists and their activities.

Fifth Member : You referred to mass movements and mass resistance to defeat the invaders. Can you prove your point by quoting some successful illustrations?

Verma: *(With a smile)* Well, Sir, we do not have to go very far. We can take the example of our own country. The British conquered India because there was no unity among those who were ruling the country and the majority of the population was indifferent and not roused politically. Then Mahatma Gandhi came on the scene and converted the independence movement into a mass movement. Credit also goes to Netaji Subhash Chandra Bose who organised Indian National Army overseas to fight the British for the liberation of the country, ultimately forcing the British to quit. Again, let us take the case of Vietnam. Neither the mighty Americans nor the huge Chinese could prevail over Vietnam because of the mass resistance put forth by the Vietnamese people. Similarly, Napoleon and Hitler could not succeed against the mass resistance of the Russian people although they won several battles. Thus it is clear that people when united can defeat any powerful enemy or invader.

Fifth Member: But this does not seem to have worked in the case of Iraq.

Verma: No doubt, the US-led coalition succeeded in subduing Iraq due to its far superior military power. It even captured, prosecuted and executed the Iraqi dictator, Saddam Hussein, yet the brave Iraqi people cannot be subjugated for all time. The sporadic suicidal bomb attacks on American and British forces, as also on members of Iraqi Governing Council had been and are still resulting in casualties far in excess of those in the actual war. It pinpoints the fact that Iraqis will not rest till they achieve their freedom back.

Fifth Member: Do you think US has surrendered to the will of Iraqi people and considers it a lost game?

Verma: Exactly Sir. The US policy regarding Iraq has failed miserably. Its Iraq policy has been equally criticised both at home and globally. That is why, Mr. Barack Obama not only became the President but has also been awarded the Nobel Peace Prize of 2009. There has to be some visible shift in the US policy.

In fact, the US wants to wriggle out of Iraq at the earliest. Appearances are deceptive. Sir, in the, long run, if the people stay united and continue the mass resistance, they are bound to win. The Americans are trying "divide and rule" policy in Iraq as the British did in India. They have set up a stooge Governing Council consisting mostly of the Kurds and the Shias. But the Iraqis are brave people and they are fighting for their sovereignty. They are sure to succeed one day. In Vietnam too, the Americans set up the South Vietnam regime. But in the long run, the people were successful in asserting themselves. Iraq too would repeat history on Vietnam's resistance pattern.

Sixth Member: What, according to you, is the main reason of China's economic progress? How was it able to stand upright in the times of global slowdown?

Verma: Sir, the main reason according to me, is China's effective financial system. Though the strength and versatility of China's financial sector has seldom been recognised, China has made a lot of progress on account of its well designed financial sector. It has three parts, each of which contributes to its overall effectiveness. The first is its market-based financial sector, the second is policy-directed lending part and the third is corporate-retained earnings and private equity contribution-based financing system.

Sixth Member: How does this three part finance system help China to grow?

Verma: China's market-based financial system has been protected from unwise investments by the country's tight management of international investment flows. Capital controls have worked well. They allow China's monetary policy to remain independent of international influences and promote a high degree of exchange rate stability and predictability. Its Government policy-led bank lending for highways, ports and other lower-return investments is also one of the reasons for China's long-term economic success. It has helped create a public space in which China's private and other competitive enterprises can do so well. And the third most important source of investment funding in China is zero-role of its banks. Corporate retained earnings and private equity contributions go to competitive, for profit companies through decisions of members and business partners. This type of financing has proved very effective and efficient.

Sixth Member: How will you define China's current economic situation in one line?

Verma: China's inflation is down and the Government has both the tools and policy position to stimulate domestic demand which enable China to face global crisis from a position of strength.

Chairman: Recently, in an interview, the leading Indian scientist, Mr. R.K. Pachauri expressed his views on climate change. What were those views?

Verma: Mr. Pachauri, who heads the Nobel Prize-winning Intergovernmental Panel on Climate Change, expressed several views regarding climate change. According to him, just a political statement has no sense. He expressed that the rich countries should commit to reducing emissions by at least 25-40 per cent. The biggest threat is the US, according to him. Except the US, most rich countries have declared targets to reduce emissions. For example, the European Union is willing to cut 30 per cent of its emissions by 2030, Japan has announced 15 per cent and Australia has also declared a plan. The biggest polluters are in North America-US and Canada. According to him, India should not accept any condition, unless rich countries declare their commitments.

Chairman: What message does the recent US insistence on India's signing the Nuclear Non-Proliferation Treaty convey?

Verma: It was not a friendly act, Sir. Nor was getting the G8 to endorse a proposed Nuclear Suppliers Group ban on the sale of enrichment and reprocessing technology to India. The Indian stand thus far has been able to accept only the safeguards and protocols of the International Atomic Energy Agency. The US insistence on limiting the number of reprocessing facilities which can be built in relation to the reactors is indeed a problem. If accepted, it will place unreasonable restriction on India's civilian reprocessing options. The fact that India has the NSG waiver under its belt means it has, though only on paper, more bargaining power than it used to have in the past.

> ***Final Comments:*** *Mr. Verma is a cheerful and pleasant candidate with a warm and friendly disposition. He is well-informed of current events as well as latest developments in various specialised fields like science, technology, art, literature, etc. He reveals the courage and capacity to express his original and candid views on national, international and personal matters without reservations or inhibitions. The special point to note on his part is his ability to present the different or opposite views in a tactful and agreeable but nevertheless firm and decisive manner. His general approach is methodical and systematic and he displays excellent ability to plan, organise, direct and coordinate tasks involving several participants. He shines as an able leader who can achieve organisation goals with remarkable success. Selected with top grading.*

Model Interview for Indian Foreign Service

Model Interview-4

Candidate, Verghese George Mathews from Kozhikode, our candidate for interview, radiates an air of cool confidence with his good carriage, firm steps, deliberate movements and polished conduct. He looks smart and well attired in his well-fitting, properly tailored dress of light colour. He enjoys a warm and cheerful disposition and his large, dark eyes reflect keenness and interest. One is able to perceive instantly in his appearance and conduct certain urge, liveliness, assurance and enthusiasm which remain the hallmarks of his personality and attraction.

The Interview ———————————————————————

Mathews: Good morning to you all Sirs.

Chairman: Good morning to you, Mr. Mathews. Please take your seat, *(He indicates the chair meant for the candidate)* Please relax and be at ease.

Mathews: Thank you, Sir. *(He occupies the chair without unnecessary movements or noise. He remains seated in an attentive manner with his mind relaxed awaiting the next observation of the Chairman.)*

Chairman: *(Smiling)* I find you have mentioned in your bio data that your interests are reading and outdoor activities. How do you reconcile these two? Am I to understand that you do all your readings outdoors? *(He laughs)*.

Mathews: I am sorry Sir and my apologies to have caused confusion. I wish to clarify that I read newspapers, magazines, periodicals, etc., regularly and also some books at least for an hour for relaxation as well as for acquiring some knowledge. However, I am also fond of outdoor activities and I indulge in them with my friends, again on a regular basis.

Chairman: Have you any favourite newspapers or magazines which you would not like to miss?

Mathews: Yes Sir. At home, we subscribe to *The Hindu* of which I am a regular reader. Our neighbours subscribe to *The Indian Express* and we exchange our newspapers. I can say I am also a regular reader of the *Indian Express*. At the college library, we get all the leading newspapers of the country and I glance through them and read any articles, editorials and other items which interest me. As for magazines and periodicals, I like *Competition Success Review, Frontline, India Today, Outlook* and the *Time* magazine. Of course, I subscribe to the *Reader's Digest*. (Since I have been going through these fairly regularly, I will certainly not want to miss). But the magazines and periodicals can be had anywhere in India.

Chairman: Now, what can you tell us about your outdoor activities?

Mathews: I should say that I spend most of my spare time or leisure hours on outdoor activities and in the company of my friends. We spend an hour in the morning for jogging and physical exercises. In the evening, we have games at the college. On Sundays and holidays, we have league cricket fixtures. Then, there are occasional picnics, cycle treks and the like. I also do not miss college excursions, NCC camps, etc. During summer vacations, we go to visit our relatives at distant places like Delhi, Kolkata, Chennai, etc.

1st Member: Can you mention some items of news or current topics which you found interesting or significant in recent weeks?

Mathews: The most important, to my mind, is the recent assertion of the United States that there is a "syndicate of terror" operating in Afghanistan-Pakistan. It now perceives this "syndicate of terror" as a threat that intends to provoke an India-Pakistan conflict and destabilise the region. The US Defence Secretary, Mr. Robert Gates, said about the terror syndicate at a press conference in New Delhi. He said that while al-Qaeda was primarily in safe havens on the Afghanistan-Pakistan border, the Taliban was active in Afghanistan and the Tehreek-e-Taliban targeted Pakistan. The Lashkare-Taiba focussed on both India and Pakistan. He admitted that it was a very complicated situation and it was dangerous for the whole region. They are a syndicate of terror, according to him and the success of any one group might lead to new capabilities and new reputation for all. He also tried to drive home the idea that targeting only one group would not lead to the elimination of the threat. The syndicate as a whole had to be fought and defeated *i.e.,* eliminated.

1st Member: Why do you find this news of such an importance? Every Indian, or Pakistani, for that matter, knows about all these terror groups very well.

Mathews: The knowledge about these groups is not very important. What makes it important is the US viewpoint which has a marked departure from the previous stand. Mr. Gates acknowledged India's restraint and statesmanship shown after the Mumbai terror attacks in November 2008. He was quite vociferous in his acknowledgment of the Indian stand and made it clear that the Indian restraint and statesmanship would be "limited", if such an event recurred. While praising India's extraordinary support to Afghanistan with New Delhi committing $1.3 billion in developmental assistance, Mr. Gates also talked of suspicion in both India and Pakistan over what the latter was doing there. He admitted that India was focussed on development, humanitarian assistance and providing limited training to the Afghan police.

1st Member: Do you think there are other important news also?

Mathews: Yes, Sir. As I think, China's economic growth is also very much important. There had been reports about China's growing economy which grew by a stunning 10.7 per cent in the fourth quarter of 20.... As newspersons reported, China might have replaced Japan as the second largest economy. While the other developed nations were still grappling with recession shocks, China clocked an economic growth rate of 8.7 per cent in 20.... China had resorted to a proactive fiscal policy and relatively eased monetary steps to keep up the growth momentum. The latest economic figures, however, have also raised concerns that China may tighten money supply in the coming months to prevent the economy from overheating. Earlier in January 20..., the Chinese central bank raised the cash reserve requirements of its banks by 50 basis points. The World Bank had forecast economy to expand 2.7 per cent in 20..., while it expected Chinese GDP to grow as much as 9 per cent in 20....

Meanwhile, the World Bank also said towards the end of January, 20... that the global economy was likely to grow at a rate of 2.7 per cent in 20..., but warned that the economic recovery was fragile. It also said that the process of recovery would gradually slow down later in 20..., as the impact of fiscal stimulus wore away.

3rd Member: Can you say something about the US stand on the Honduras election?

Mathews: Yes, Sir, I can. The Honduras presidential election in the last week of November 20... was a brazen attempt to legitmise the military coup that ousted the democratically elected President Manuel Zelaya in June 20.... The Barack Obama administration in the US, was quick to give the November election the stamp of legitimacy. What is to be noticed is that after the June military coup, the US had, after initial hesitation, added its voice to the international condemnation that had followed. With the others, it had also demanded the restoration of Mr. Zelaya to the presidency. But everything became clear in the months that followed. The US backtracked on its commitments to restore democracy and the rule of law in the Central American union.

3rd Member: Do you want to suggest that the Honduran Government survived because of the US support?

Mathews: Exactly, Sir. The isolated, military backed Honduran Government must have collapsed, had it not had the tacit support of the US. Actually, the US has set up its largest military base there in Latin America. Besides, it is common knowledge that the Honduran army is trained and armed by the US. In addition, the Honduran economy is entirely dependent on the US support. Given these circumstances, it becomes quite clear that the Obama administration, despite the inherent illegitimacy of the electoral exercise, hailed the results as a very important step forward for Honduras. In addition, it called the election a legitimate way out of the crisis that had engulfed the country after the military coup.

3rd Member: Was there any other step that made clear that the US was giving a stamp of legitimacy to the election?

Mathews: Of course, Sir. The US had sent election observers under the auspices of the International Republican Institute and the National Democratic Institute for International Affairs, a move that showed the bipartisan support the coup-makers had come to enjoy in Washington. Both the organisations are supported by the National Endowment for Democracy (NED). The NED was an enthusiastic backer of the 20... coup attempt in Venezuela and the colour revolutions in Eastern Europe as well.

3rd Member: How was this election held? Was there any protest?

Mathews: The so-called fair and free election was held under the shadow of the gun. Since the coup in June 20..., the military had been riding roughshod over the trade union groups and poor neighbourhoods. This actually constituted Mr. Zelaya's main support base. On the election day, 40,000 troops had been mobilised to frighten the electorate. This broke up the rallies that were protesting against the election. People were, in fact, forced to cast their vote at many places. The military-backed government also told citizens that the boycott of election would be considered an illegal act. That is why, the National Front against the coup, an umbrella group of three main trade unions, human rights organisations and women's groups, called this election a fraudulent exercise.

2nd Member: What do you think about the jurisdiction of High Courts?

Mathews: The Constitution of India does not attempt detailed definitions and classification of the different types of jurisdiction of the High Courts. It has, however, done so clearly in the case of Supreme Court. This is mainly because most of the High Courts, at the time of the framing of the Constitution, had been functioning with well defined jurisdictions, whereas the Supreme Court was a newly-created institution necessitating a clear definition of its powers and functions. The Constitution, however, vests four additional powers in the High Courts, apart from the normal original and appellate jurisdiction. These are:

1. the power to issue writs or orders for the enforcement of the Fundamental Rights or for any other purpose;

2. the power of superintendence over all courts in the State;

3. the power to transfer cases to itself from subordinate courts concerning the interpretation of the Constitution; and

4. the power to appoint officers and staff of the High Court.

4th Member: What do you understand by vertical and horizontal nuclear proliferation? Which of the two, in your opinion, is more dangerous that the NPT aims to control?

Mathews : Vertical nuclear proliferation relates to more and more stockpiling of nuclear weapons and devices with higher and higher destructive capacity, by the existing nuclear nations. Horizontal proliferation refers to acquisition of nuclear weapons capability by non-nuclear powers of today. To my mind, horizontal proliferation is more dangerous. If countries like Iran, Iraq, Libya, etc. acquire nuclear capability, they may start a nuclear war which would ultimately threaten this planet itself. It does not mean that vertical proliferation is not dangerous but for many decades the nuclear deterrent appears to have averted the Third World War. At this point of time, the countries seem to be moving towards disarmament evidenced by various steps taken by the world community. The NPT aims to stop horizontal nuclear proliferation.

4th Member: India strongly supports disarmament and total ban on nuclear weapons. Why then it is not subscribing to the NPT?

Mathews: *(Smiling)* As you correctly said Sir, India is all set for total ban on nuclear weapons. Unfortunately NPT does not at all subscribe to the total ban. It allows the Big Five not only to possess but also to further develop nuclear weapons, in other words, permitting vertical nuclear proliferation. China is a nuclear power and it taught us a bitter lesson in 1962 when we neglected our military build up. Now, with its nuclear capability, it can hold us to ransom again and we will be at the mercy of China. To avoid such a contingency, we have acquired nuclear capability on our own without external aid by conducting the Pokhran nuclear explosions. Since the NPT is discriminatory and makes us vulnerable, we are right in not signing the same.

5th Member: What is Maoism? How did it come to be known so?

Mathews: Sir, what has come to be known as Maoism had, in fact, its roots in China's economic backwardness. It was a result of the failure of Chinese Communist Party in the urban areas in the 1920s. It subsequently gave birth to peasant-cum-guerrilla-based movement in the countryside. Mao constantly applied Marx's materialist dialectics in helping to understand and resolve multiple contradictions-internal conflicts tending to split what is functionally united-with the likely outcome following from the reciprocal actions of the opposing tendencies. Actually, we can say, Maoism implies learning truth from practice like Marxism, at its best, it is a comprehensive world view, a method of analysis and a guide to practice, not a set of dogmas.

5th Member: In view of global warming or climate change, alternative sources of energy have become important. Do you think solar energy has any potential for a country like ours?

Mathews : Yes, Sir. I think so. Solar energy has the estimated physical potential *i.e.,* 94 per cent of India's additional electricity needs by 2031-32. In addition, solar energy can leapfrog grid extension. Its employment multiplier is greater than other forms of renewable energy. It can really add to national energy security. Its cost per unit is thought to be comparable to or less than that of electricity from coal and oil-fuelled generating stations once their externalities and current subsidies are factored in.

5th Member: What has India achieved as far as production of solar energy is concerned?

Mathews: Solar energy, at present, supplies only 0.75 per cent of India's electricity. Just 5 per cent of the Ministry of New and Renewable Energy budget is devoted to solar energy under the Five-Year Plan. In contrast, fossil fuel-based electricity generation had a very large set of public support measures and subsidies-averaging 150 per cent of the capital costs of projects between 20... and 20.... . Since over the half of the population still does not have access to any form of electricity, the Indian subsidy, as a whole, is socially regressive. It benefits the upper income groups at the expense of poor people and those living in backward regions. I think, it is in both the national and the global public interest that India develop solar as well as other sources of renewable energy.

6th Member: What accounts for the high rate of literacy in Kerala, which is your native State, though it has dwindled slightly?

Mathews: I would say that the influence of Christianity in Kerala has contributed to a great extent for the high rate of literacy in Kerala. Christianity came very early to Kerala, may be in the very first century AD itself. The Christian missionaries started many schools and played a significant role in spreading education. Thus, Kerala had an early start and education was not confined only to the higher castes. Secondly part of present Kerala State was in the Madras Presidency of the British period and enjoyed better educational facilities.

> **Comments:** *The candidate shows excellent understanding of current national and international events and trends. He is aware of latest developments in this field and there is sound logic and reasoning in his arguments.*

Model Interviews for Indian Police Service

Model Interview-5

Miss Mona Bhattacharjee is a charming and attractive candidate of average height, lean build, fair complexion, sharp features. Dressed in a saree she looks elegant and dignified.

The Interview____

Mona: *(With a cheerful and warm smile playing on her lips, enters the room and salutes the Board with an exquisite 'namaste'. Her whole action reveals grace, courtesy and finesse.)* Namaste to you all, Sirs.

Chairman: Namaste, Miss Bhattacharjee. Please sit down. *(He indicates the chair meant for the candidate).*

Mona: Thank you, Sir. *(She sits down smartly with minimum of movements and noise. When seated she looks relaxed* *and comfortable but remains alert to hear the next observation of the Chairman or other Members.)*

Chairman: Miss Mona, I find that you had stayed throughout in the college and university hostels during your college and university education. Is it because you felt you could concentrate more on studies if you stayed in the hostel instead of at home?

Mona: *(Smiling cheerfully and pleasantly)* Sir, initially I joined the hostel out of necessity. As you could see, my father is in military service. I did my Higher Secondary in Delhi where my father was then stationed. My parents felt Delhi University is best suited for my college education and I joined the Indraprastha College for my B.A. (Hons.) course. Soon after that my father was transferred to the Eastern Sector and I had to move into the college hostel. Having joined the hostel, I found it had its own advantages. I did enjoy the hostel life and it was real fun. Practically, all hostel inmates became my friends. As for concentrating on studies, it depends on one's will power, involvement and determination. *(Smiling)* I could concentrate on my studies irrespective of whether I stay at home or in the hostel.

Chairman: What, in your experience, have been the major advantages of staying in the hostel?

Mona: I already mentioned the most important one. It helps one to make a large number of new friends. Secondly, you save valuable time since commuting by bus between home and college is very time-consuming indeed. Next, you can make full use of the sports facilities available in the college and hostel complex. Thanks to my stay in the hostel I could become the champion swimmer and diver of the university, attain good proficiency in tennis and also win the college athletics championship prize. Lastly, I could fully avail of the college and university library facilities. The greatest advantage is to consult seniors for any problem in studies. Like comrades, they are always at hand to guide you. Further, away from day-to-day social obligations, you can concentrate on your studies much better. You see, it has helped me to accomplish the goals I set for myself when I joined the college.

Chairman: What were your goals?

Mona: I wanted to do well in studies and also in sports. To be specific, in studies I wanted to get a first division and a position within the first ten places. As regards sports, I wanted to become the champion swimmer and diver of the university.

Chairman: Well, you have accomplished your aims. You have scored first division throughout and in M.A., you have secured the second rank in the university. So also in sports you have done well. Now, what is your goal with regard to your career?

Mona: *(Smiling)* I am here, Sir, in pursuit of my career goal. I had made up my mind to get into the IPS for my career and my aim is to top the merit list. It is a challenging task and I have been concentrating my efforts to achieve this goal. I am confident of success.

1st Member: Would you attribute success to hard work and persistent effort or to luck or chance?

Mona: *(Once again smiles as she answers)* I believe in hard work and determined sustained effort. While I persist with my effort, I am aware that fulfilment will come with the grace of God or luck. But without my effort, luck favouring me is remote and I certainly do not gamble on it. Luck also favours the brave, I mean the people who put their shoulders to wheels to achieve their cherished goal

1st Member: Many film stars have become great celebrities overnight because of luck. Some time back a poor man in Tamil Nadu became a crorepati when he won the two-crore-rupee prize in a raffle. That is also sheer luck.

Mona: *(Smiles)* Perhaps you have something there. But I feel talent, hard work, perseverance and determination are indispensable for lasting success. The film stars must also have put in hard work. The winner of the two crore rupees' lottery said in an interview that he had been buying lottery tickets for over 10 years. The Indian philosophy says that good or ill luck in this life is the fruit of one's past 'karma' or deeds. This again means effort bearing fruit at some future point of time.

1st Member: Do you want to suggest that it is one's past "karma" which decides everything?

Mona: No Sir. Actually, I have referred to the common notion. As far as my personal views are concerned, I again say that for every gain, 90 per cent of labour matters and only 10 per cent is left to chance or luck. Winning the two-crore rupee prize goes in favour of luck, even if he had been buying lottery tickets for last ten years. I agree, but stray incidents cannot be taken as an example. For example, a human being is born with two hands and two legs. If someone is born with three legs, it cannot be quoted in support of any point. Something that can be applied to the majority is a truth and those truths that involve very rare persons present no example in such cases.

2nd Member: You have chosen Economics as one of your Optional subjects. As a student of Economics, would you say that India's economy is conditioned by the vagaries of monsoon?

Mona: Sir, unlike the industrialised countries of the West, Indian economy is essentially agriculture-oriented. As much as 65 per cent of the population is engaged in agricultural activities. Bulk of our agricultural output is dependent on monsoon rains. River water and well water irrigation is limited. Hence, it is true that monsoon has a say on our economic output and growth rate. But we need not be totally dependent on monsoon. We must avail of modern science and technology to minimise the monsoon effects.

2nd Member: Can you elaborate further and explain how modern methods can help?

Mona: First of all, while there is drought in some areas, we have floods elsewhere. In Assam, floods are a regular annual feature. If we have the Ganga-Cauvery canal built, the flood waters could be used advantageously in drought areas. Besides, as you are aware, Sir, the implementation of mega project of interlinking rivers of North and South India at a cost of ₹ 5,60,000 crore was undertaken during the previous NDA regime. A high-powered committee had also been constituted to undertake the feasibility of the project. Another method is rain harvesting, which was successfully demonstrated through rejuvenating the Arvari river in Rajasthan with the construction of a series of check dams along the slopes of the Aravallis. Next is the storage of water. There are modern methods to slow down evaporation. Our lakes, tanks, etc. can be made a lot more deeper to store more water. Modern techniques can be usefully employed to pump out subsoil water. Satellite weather forecasting and statistical analysis could give more accurate predictions regarding monsoon occurrences. Agricultural research can help to achieve short-term, quick yielding, less water dependent crops. We should go in for all these and other similar techniques. We can also adopt drip irrigation in rain-scarce areas.

2nd Member: I see, you are talking of modern techniques. Can you elaborate on Remote Sensing and Geographical Information System?

Mona: Yes, I can Sir. Remote Sensing and Geographical Information System are accepted as effective tools in water resources development and management to complement and supplement ground data. Space borne remote sensing data provide timely and reliable information on available water resources and its utilisation. Remote sensing inputs have been significantly contributing to water management in India, both in its conservation and control aspects. From its modest beginning with surface water inventory, satellite remote sensing technology has progressed to more complex management in the field of snow hydrology, reservoir sedimentation assessment, irrigation water management, hydrological studies, flood management, interlinking of rivers, snow and glacier studies, hydropower project, command area development, Water Resources Information System (WRIS), Accelerated Irrigation Benefit

Programmes (AIBP), monitoring of water logging and salinity areas and watershed monitoring.

2nd Member: What is the advantage of using remote sensing data?

Mona: The main advantage of using remote sensing data for hydrological modelling and monitoring is its ability to generate information in spatial and temporal domains.

3rd Member: A news has been doing rounds that the signing of Kerry-Lugar Bill has widened the gulf between the military and the civilian dispensation in Pakistan. What do you think?

Mona: The dust has settled over the Kerry-Lugar Bill to a great extent. But the debate triggered by the conditions in the legislation-strengthening democratic forces in Pakistan did not achieve its objective. Strengthening democratic forces means that Pakistan should ensure that it does not aid militants who carry out terrorist acts against India and other countries and also ensure civilian control over the military and non-proliferation. Actually, there was a one-month long hysteria in Pakistan over the Bill, after it was already passed by the Congress. It resulted in drastically changing the civil-military balance in the favour of the military. It, in fact, left the democratically elected Pakistan People's Party-led government considerably weaker.

3rd Member: Do you want to say, the Pakistan Army is still more powerful than the government?

Mona : Yes Sir, exactly. The protests against the Bill shattered the nerves of the Pakistani government and served to isolate its head as well.

3rd Member: Do the people in general prefer the military rule to the civilian rule in Pakistan?

Mona: At least from the developments in the last 20 months of the Pak rule suggests so. The KLB fiasco, as this signing of the Bill has been referred to, can be seen as a positive proof of such a perception. There have been several instances of the erosion of the authority of the elected government. With some exceptions, even the Pakistani media which apparently oppose the military rule, made explicit remarks about their endorsement of a military rule. They said that the government was stupid when it allowed the US to impose the conditions that left no choice for Pakistan. It brought to the fore even Nawaz Sharif's Pakistan Muslim League's real intentions. Despite his tall claims of supporting the government to keep the military subservient to civil rule, his party chose to oppose a US Bill that wanted exactly this.

4th Member: Some, intellectuals and analysts have been reiterating that the West must not undermine Myanmar's people. What do they actually mean?

Mona: Actually, the question has arisen out of the positive signals from the ruling military Junta. But we cannot presume any change of heart. There are, in fact, several reasons for the regime's shifting stance. One is that the Junta has begun to recognise that it needs the legitimacy that only a relatively transparent poll process can bring. The creation of regional legislatures may help defuse ongoing, historically violent tensions with the country's 16 ethnic groups domestically. But internationally, only a respectable election can trigger an easing of sanctions and additional aid and investment. Actually, the Senior-General Than Shwe, the head of the ruling Junta wants to secure his legacy by regularising Myanmar's relations with the West. Analysts and intellectuals actually want the Western policy to be calibrated to strengthen, not undermine the legitimate aspirations of the Myanmarese people.

4th Member: Why is such a change taking place in the ruling Junta's stance?

Mona: The change in the Junta's approach might be the outcome of the US President Mr. Barack Obama's willingness to reopen the dialogue. Another reason may be the desire to counter China's growing influence. Harsh words from Beijing over the forced exodus of 30,000 mostly ethnic Chinese Burmese from Kokang into Yunnan province came as a sharp reminder that China, traditionally, was Myanmar's No. 1 enemy. Its security and commercial interests do not necessarily coincide with Yangoon's.

4th Member: What will be the nature of the 20... election in Myanmar?

Mona: The 20... election is bound to prove problematic. Myanmar's new Constitution guarantees the continuing ascendancy of the military. New political candidates and parties will be vetted, Iran style. Lack of free media, the absence of independent scrutiny, and intolerance of open debate do not favour the holding of free and fair polls.

5th Member: Has NAM any future after the disintegration of USSR, and USA emerging as the only 'superpower'?

Mona: No doubt, with the emergence of US as the only 'superpower' both militarily and economically, the Cold War era is over (even the mighty USSR, now shrunk to Russian Federation, is looking to it for economic reconstruction) and NAM as a political force has lost much of its utility. It could not effectively check the unjustified attack by the US-led coalition forces on Iraq. Yet in the economic sphere, NAM has still a role. G8, G20 etc., have been contemplating to bring burning problems under control and phasing out the undesirable elements in an organised way. There is a need for collective efforts by all the 116 members of NAM to safeguard their economic interest and change the global economic geography in their favour. I think it is right time for India to give a lead to NAM, being one of the founding fathers along with Egypt and erstwhile Yugoslavia 48 years back in 1961.

Chairman: What is the "Financial Emergency?" In what circumstances such 'Emergency' is declared?

Mona: If the President is sure that a situation has arisen whereby the financial stability or credit of India or any part of it is threatened, he or she may declare a financial emergency under Article 360. The proclamation in this case should be approved by Parliament as in the other two cases of emergency War emergency and Constitutional emergency in the States. During the financial emergency, "The executive authority of the Union shall extend to the giving of directions to any State to observe such canons of financial propriety as may be specified in the direction or any other directions which the President may deem necessary for the purpose. Such directions may include those requiring the reduction of salaries and allowances of Government servants and even those of the Judges of the Supreme Court and the High Courts."

> ***Comments:*** *A brilliant and capable candidate who enjoys all-round distinctions. She displays excellent initiative and commendable originality in answering questions and solving problems. She is able to argue her case with conviction and present her views forcefully, coherently and very convincingly. Her bold and pragmatic approach coupled with sincerity and earnestness enables her to influence others to her way of thinking.*

Model Interview-6

Mr. M. Kapoor is ushered in. He enters the room and offer his salutation to the chairman and the members. When asked to take his seat, he gets seated and thanks the Chairman with a pleasant and warm smile.

The Interview

Chairman: Well, Mr. Kapoor you have been a student of Science, how is it that you have chosen to join the I.P.S.?

Mr. M. Kapoor: Although science has been my hobby, Sir, I studied Science only upto Intermediate standard and, because I want to lead a life of action and adventure, so I have chosen to join Police Service.

Chairman: Do you read daily newspapers?

Mr. M. Kapoor: Yes Sir, I read the Hindu regularly.

Chairman: Why do you prefer the Hindu?

Mr. M. Kapoor: Sir, I like the Hindu mainly for its wide coverage. It is a big newspaper publishing news in detail—all types of news, political, social economic, cultural, games and sports, trade and commerce, science & technology besides all sorts of advertisements. It provides window to all current news, national and international. Besides, its editorials on important topics particularly on controversial ones are impartial, balanced and unbiased.

Chairman: What periodicals or magazines do you read regularly?

Chairman: Sir, I read the Frontline and the India Today.

First Member: What games do you like most and play Mr. Kapoor.

Mr. Kapoor: Football is my favourite game, Sir, and during my final year at the college I was the captain of the University eleven. I also play Cricket and Tennis.

First Member: Supposing, as a captain you are one of the selectors of the University team and you have to select a player for the left-extreme position. You have two good players: one of them is an able dribbler and can dodge even the best of defenders. The other chap is good in passing the ball and he could kick with ease with both feet. Whom would you prefer and why?

Mr. Kapoor: Sir, I would go in for the second chap who could kick with both feet and could put the ball well. As a left-extreme you are not good if you cannot kick with your left leg and the ability to kick with both feet will help you to pass the ball in any direction and surprise the opponents. On the other hand, the dribbler will be a marked man and could be bottled up and rendered ineffective. Finally the game of football is team work and the dribbler may give precedence to his solo effort over the team's requirements. We need co-operation, understanding and team spirit rather than individual skill that alone will not help the team in winning.

First Member: Since you are tied up with football all the time and so much, how could you find time to play cricket?

Mr. Kapoor: Generally, the football matches are played in the evening during week days. On the other hand, the cricket practice and matches are played generally on Sundays and holidays. Besides, the seasons for both the games are also different. During the cricket season there is not much of football.

Second Member: Have you taken part in debates or elocution contests or similar extra-curricular activities, Mr. Kapoor?

Mr. Kapoor: Yes Sir, I represented my college twice in the intercollegiate debates. We won the rolling cup the second time and I was fortunate enough to win the best speaker's cup on both the occasions. As for the extra-curricular activities, I was the Secretary of the College Students Union for one year and organised various union activities. I have also taken part in the amateur dramas staged by the college and in radio plays.

Second Member: On what subject did you speak when you won the rolling cup?

Mr. Kapoor: Sir, the topic was "Going nuclear will do more harm than good to India at the present juncture" and I opposed the motion. Frankly, Sir, I very strongly feel that the sooner India becomes a nuclear power the better it is for herself and also for the world. A nation's biggest capital is its strength by virtue of which it can earn regard and respect of all nations and can ensure its defence against desperadoes.

Second Member: Why do you think so, Mr. Kapoor?

Mr. Kapoor: You can see Sir, what happened to China. If China had not acquired the nuclear capacity and had also not developed the ability to put her own satellite around the earth, do you think that America would have allowed it to enter the U.N., and that President Nixon would have made the Pilgrimage to Beijing and paid obeissance to Mao Tse Tung? No one would have bothered about China if it had not developed the nuclear potential and mastered the satellite technology. Britain handed over Hong Kong to China and wishes to have friendly relations with her. Recently the President of China, visited the U.S.A., the President of the U.S.A., accorded to him a warm welcome and treated him as a leader of a great country. It is certainly because of the fact that China is a great military power. One has but to read Chinese history before the Communist revolution to find that a weak China had to suffer humiliation at the hands of the imperial powers. In my opinion, no one will take serious notice of India until she conclusively demonstrates that she is a power to reckon with.

Third Member: You have been a student of Psychology?

Mr. Kapoor: Yes Sir, it was one of my subjects in B.A.

Third Member: How does the study of Psychology help an I.P.S. officer?

Mr. Kapoor: It helps a lot, Sir. The study of Psychology is greatly helpful in detecting crimes. Criminology is largely based on psychology.

Third Member: What do you understand by third degree methods?

Mr. Kapoor: The use of terror and violence in interrogating criminals is known as third degree methods. This method is not permitted by law. But the police generally terrorise the criminals mercilessly to make them confess their crime.

Third Member: What is your opinion about this method?

Mr. Kapoor: I can only say that in an ideal society there should be no place for third degree methods. Under this method people are forced to admit or confess crimes which they might have never done. A person should be treated as innocent unless his crime is proved without any doubt. Generally, the accused accepts the guilt when he is in police custody but denies it when he appears before the judicial officer in a court of law. The court also does not take cognisance of what the accused had said or written when he was in police lock-up.

Third Member: Have you heard about Scotland Yard?

Mr. Kapoor: Yes Sir. Scotland Yard is the name of the Police Head Quarters of the United Kingdom. The intelligence officers of the Scotland Yard are known all-over the world for their efficiency in detecting crimes.

Third Member: Do you know about the Chambal ravines?

Mr. Kapoor: Yes Sir, they are in Madhya Pradesh near Gwalior and are notorious for the hideouts of dacoits.

Third Member: Tell something about the plan of the Sarvodaya leaders to liquidate the dacoits?

Mr. Kapoor: Many years ago Vinoba Bhave visited the ravines and appealed to the dacoits to come out of their hideouts and surrender to the government and turn a new leaf in their lives.

Third Member: How far did his appeal succeed?

Mr. Kapoor: Subsequently other Sarvodaya leaders also visited the area, contacted the dacoits and conveyed to them the message of Vinoba.

Third Member: What is your opinion about the Sarvodaya approach to the problem of the dacoits?

Mr. Kapoor: It is a very ticklish question. Sir and I am unable to give a mature answer to this question. Yet I am inclined to agree that Vinoba's is a correct approach. It should be the aim of society to convert the criminals to good citizens. If we go through the history of some of the criminals we would discover that they were good citizens but an outrageous act at a particular period compelled them to commit a crime. This leads to repetition of crimes till they become hardened criminals. If they are treated leniently we can still hope that they would lead a good life.

Third Member: Have you heard of the sandal wood smuggler Veerappan in Karnataka who dodged the State police for several years. He was responsible for hundreds of murders, innumerable kidnappings and other crimes. It was with great diffculty that he was caught and killed. What is your opinion regarding such cases?

Mr. Kapoor: Sir, such things happen because of a variety of factors, the most important of which is political patronage. It is due to this that even great offenders succeed in evading being caught and punished. If we really want to stamp out crime, it is imperative that the criminals are treated as criminals and no political shelter is provided to them.

Fourth Member: What is your hobby, Mr. Kapoor.

Mr. Kapoor: My hobby is gardening, Sir. We have a small kitchen garden at the rear of our house. We also have a lawn with some flowerbeds in front of the house. My father is also interested in gardening. We work in our garden during our leisure hours. In the front garden we have roses and other seasonal flower plants. In the kitchen garden we grow vegetables.

Fourth Member: Well, Mr. Kapoor that is all. The interview is over.

Mr. Kapoor: Thank you Sir.

> *Comments: The candidate is well informed about the latest developments. He is methodical and systematic in planning and organising task and their implementation. He is very rational regarding issues of national importance.*

Model Interview for Indian Forest Service

Model Interview-7

Mr. Anup Singh is a candidate for Indian Forest Service. He looks smart and confident with pleasant personality. Rays of success are clearly viewed on his face. When called, he enters the interview room and greets all the members along with the chairperson.

The Interview____

Mr. Singh: Good morning, Sirs.

Chairman: Good Morning, Mr. Anup Singh.

Chairman: From which college did you graduate, Mr. Singh?

Mr. Singh: From the Government Agricultural College, Amritsar.

Chairman: What is your hobby?

Mr. Singh: My hobby is Study of Nature, Sir.

Chairman: Have you ever used a microscope?

Mr. Singh: Certainly, very often in the course of my science practical work.

Chairman: Do you think that a microscope is the chief ally of the scientists?

Mr. Singh: It is certainly one of the chief aids on which a scientist must rely.

Chairman: What sort of timber is used for railway sleepers in India?

Mr. Singh: I think it is chiefly sal and teak.

Chairman: Where does most of it come from?

Mr. Singh: Teak from the forests of Madhya Pradesh, Maharashtra, Tamil Nadu, Karnataka and Kerala while sal from those of Uttar Pradesh, Assam, Bihar and Orissa.

Chairman: Where do you have the Deodar type of forests?

Mr. Singh: These are hill forests which are chiefly found in the elevated regions of the Himalayas at altitudes from 5,000 to 10,000 feet and with a rainfall ranging from 100 to 250 cm.

Chairman: And where do we have the arid forests?

Mr. Singh: Sir, these are found in Rajasthan and dry regions of Uttar Pradesh in the north, and in the dry tracts of the Deccan specially where the rainfall is 25 to 75 cm.

Chairman: Mr. Singh, could you please tell us when was the Forest Service founded in India?

Mr. Singh: Sir, the foundation of Forest Service in India was laid in 1865 with the appointment of the first Inspector-General of Forests.

Chairman: Was it then under the control of the Provincial Governments?

Mr. Singh: No, Sir, it was then administered by the Central Government. At present, however, it is under the control of the State Governments.

Chairman: Can you tell us when was the first forest legislation enacted?

Mr. Singh: I don't remember the exact year, Sir, I think the first piece of forest legislation was enacted in the middle of the nineteenth century.

Chairman: Do you remember its scope?

Mr. Singh: Yes Sir. This entrusted to the local governments the task of framing rules and regulation for preservation of the state forests.

Member: Well, where are the Forest Research Institutes located in India?

Mr. Singh: We have Forest Research Institutes at Dehradun and Coimbatore.

Chairman: When were these founded?

Mr. Singh: I do not remember exactly, Sir, I think it was founded a little after the enactment of the first piece of legislation regarding forests.

Chairman: Can you tell us something more about this Institute?

Mr. Singh: The Forest Research Institute at Dehradun is now known all over the world. It is under the control of the Ministry of Agriculture. The Institute conducts research on problems connected with improving, protecting and developing of forests in India, It has four museums for all those who are interested in forestry.

Member: Is there any other forest institute also?

Mr. Singh: Yes, Sir, there is one at Coimbatore in Tamil Nadu. But this is also under the control of the Central Government.

Member: Why is forest preservation necessary in India?

Mr. Singh: It is because forest preservation helps us in preventing soil erosion.

Member: What is, in your opinion, the main cause of the spread of the Rajputana desert?

Mr. Singh: In the first place, much is due to the scarcity of water and lack of irrigation in the areas in which it is spreading, but much of it is also due to the large herds of goats in these areas who eat away whatever vegetation is there and the lands denuded of the vegetation are easily ravaged by strong winds which sweep away the soil, thus causing the slow advance of the desert into the adjoining states.

Member: What steps have the Government taken to prevent this all?

Mr. Singh: The Governments are taking measures for protection and afforestation of the north-west slopes of the Aravalli Hills, creation of wind belts on either bank of the Luni, afforestation of the now barren region between the Luni and the Aravallis, fixation of the sands at the mount of the Luni with the Rann of Kutch, afforestation of the banks of the Baves river, fixation of sands on seaboards of Kathiawar and Kutch, etc.

Member: Do you think this will be sufficient to halt the desert or desert conditions in that part of the country?

Mr. Singh: Sir, this is only preliminary working of the scheme. It will be a long arduous and costly affair. The full scheme is spread over 20 years with an estimated cost of crores of rupees. At the end of that period, fresh measures will be taken for new schemes.

Chairman: What steps, do you suggest, should be taken to check soil erosion?

Mr. Singh: Sir, this is a big problem in our country, and requires much careful planning and extensive survey work before effective measures can be taken up. Such a survey should demarcate erosion-affected areas, bring out the character and degree of erosion damage there and indicate broadly the measures needed to tackle the erosion problems. In a country as large as ours with its great contrasts in topography, soils and climate, the nature of erosion problems and the measures necessary to tackle them would vary greatly in different parts.

Chairman: You seem to know the magnitude of the problem but what broad preliminary measures do you suggest should be taken to begin with?

Mr. Singh: I would suggest that measures must be taken first to restrict grazing and felling of trees for the protection of forests on hill slopes. Next I would suggest afforestation as the most suitable initial measure, specially in catchment areas, and then all-round action for dealing with gullies and ravines, where the washing away of the surface soil brings in its wake tonnes of sand, pebbles and boulders which turn extensive cultivable lands in the plains into veritable sand hidden deserts. Though the result may not be quick, I am sure the labour and expense on these measures will be fully compensated by the achieved results.

Chairman: What other measures can you suggest in the direction of soil conservation work?

Mr. Singh: Sir, for conservation all other steps that I can suggest are that CHO training, contour trenching and bunding, check damming, contour ploughing and levelling of eroded lands with the help of bulldozers should be vigorously pushed through. These anti-erosion operations will most surely go a long way to meet the menace of soil erosion and conserve it.

Chairman: That's all, Mr. Singh. Thank you.

Mr. Singh: Thank you, Sir.

> **Comments:** *The candidate displays excellent awareness in various fields. He enjoys abundant common sense and self-confidence and meets all the challenges with determination, tact and resourcefulness.*

Model Interview-8

Mr. Shyam has a quality of good Forest Officer in abundant degree like physical vigour and energy, a love of open air and country, good horsemanship etc. He enters the interview room with confidence and a pleasant smile.

The Interview____

Mr. Shyam: Good Morning, Sirs.

Chairman: Good Morning Mr. Shyam. Please take your seat.

Mr. Shyam: Thank You, Sir.

Chairman: Which part of the country do you come from?

Mr. Shyam: From Ropar in Punjab, Sir.

Chairman: What, in your opinion, has been the effect of partition on the forest resources of your State?

Mr. Shyam: The State of divided Punjab in India has practically been deprived of all its forest resources. Changamanga forests, now in Pakistan, were the chief forest resources of the State.

Chairman: And which industry has been affected adversely by this?

Mr. Shyam: Sports industry for which Sialkot was famous all over the World.

Chairman: Can you tell us some of India's forest products?

Mr. Shyam: The major products of Indian forests are fuel and timber woods, minor products which include gums and resins, lac, essential oils, fatty oils, medicinal plants, bamboos, bees' wax and honey, dyeing and tanning substances, etc.

Chairman: Which trees are of commercial importance?

Mr. Shyam: Mango, babool, sundari, rosewood, oak, neem, teak, deodar.

Chairman: Which are the oil trees and where are they found in India?

Mr. Shyam: Some of the oil trees are sandalwood or *Chandan* trees. These trees are found mostly in Southern India namely in Karnataka, Nilgiri hills, Western Ghats and Coorg. But some oils are also extracted from the seeds and nuts of various trees.

Member: In which parts of the country are canes and bamboos mostly found, and which industries are connected with them?

Mr. Shyam: Canes and bamboos are chiefly found in the Southern Konkan and Coromandal coasts, Madhya Pradesh, West Bengal, Eastern Nepal, Assam and Bhutan. Cane wood is mostly used for making baskets, mats, ropes and walking sticks. It is one of the most useful raw materials for the manufacture of paper.

Member: Which is the biggest forest state?

Mr. Shyam: Madhya Pradesh, Sir.

Member: Does India enjoy monopoly in any particular forest industry?

Mr. Shyam: Yes Sir, India enjoys a monopoly in lac trade.

Member: Well, Mr. Kohli, do you know anything about the FAO?

Mr. Shyam: It is an organisation of the United Nations for the Food and Agricultural work. It was launched after the Second World War. It took its birth from the United Nations' Conference on Food and Agriculture convened by President Roosevelt in 1943.

Member: What are the ideals before this organisation?

Mr. Shyam: This organisation aims at dealing with such problems as forest and fishery, agriculture and food. The constitution of the FAO came into being in October 1945, immediately after the termination of World War II.

Member: Who is its Director-General?

Mr. Shyam: Mr..................

Member: What help is this organisation rendering to India?

Mr. Shyam: Sir, this organisation is financing numerous schemes of technical help to our country in her drive towards self-sufficiency in food.

Member: Can you now tell us how the forests are being administered?

Mr. Shyam: Sir, the various States have been divided into one or more forest circles, each in the charge of a conservator of forest. These circles have been sub-divided into Forest Divisions in charge of officers of the superior services. These Divisions have again been sub-divided into Ranges, under the charge of trained officers called Rangers, with Foresters of Forest-Guards working under them.

Chairman: Mr. Shyam, can you ride a horse?

Mr. Shyam: Yes Sir, I am very fond of horse-riding.

Chairman: When do you get up in the morning?

Mr. Shyam: I get up at 5 am in the summer and at 6 am in winter.

Chairman: What do you do between 5 am and 8 am?

Mr. Shyam: I take a cold bath and having performed puja, I go for a brisk walk and take my breakfast on my return.

Chairman: Very well, Mr. Shyam, you may go now.

Mr. Shyam: Thank you, Sir.

> ***Comments:*** *The candidate is sincere and earnest in his approach and believes in hard work and systematic effort to achieve positive results. He has a cheerful and optimistic personality which will be useful in achieving goals.*

Model Interview for Engineering Services

Model Interview-9

Mr. Gaurav has passed the examination of combined Engineering Services and is called for the interview. He is a young energetic and pleasant person full of self-confidence. He enters the room and greets all the members along with the chairperson.

The Interview____

Mr. Gaurav: Good Morning, Sirs.

Chairman: Good Morning, Mr. Gaurav please take your seat.

Mr. Gaurav: Thank you, sir *(after taking seat).*

Chairman: In your application you have mentioned that you have passed the electrical engineering course from the Banaras Hindu University. Did you get any practical training there or thereafter.

Mr. Gaurav: Yes Sir, I have done the practical training.

Chairman: What sort of a practical training did they give you?

Mr. Gaurav: We had to work in the college workshops and we were attached to firms producing electrical goods, and with firms of repute who gave us training as apprentices.

Chairman: Can you name one?

Mr. Gaurav: Messrs Kirloskars, Mumbai.

Chairman: How many marks did you obtain in your B.E./B.Tech?

Mr. Gaurav: I got a second class with 380 marks.

Chairman: What was your position in the university?

Mr. Gaurav: Seventh, Sir.

Chairman: Are you interested only in Electrical Engineering or anything else also?

Mr. Gaurav: Electrical Engineering was my compulsory subject in which I got special training, but we were also given all-round training in other engineering branches, so I can be employed anywhere the government may require my services, though I will do well in the branch for which I got the special training.

Member: What is a turbine?

Mr. Gaurav: It is an engine that converts force of moving water (also of air or steam) into mechanical energy capable of doing work.

Member: Well Mr. Gaurav, can you give an idea of the Government of India's major irrigation projects?

Mr. Gaurav: India has a fund of water resources. If they can all be tapped to their full, the country's trumps can very easily be changed. With that motive in view, the Government of India is building several canals by erecting dams, etc., at suitable places of our various rivers.

Chairman: Will you please now tell us what is a multi-purpose project?

Mr. Gaurav: Among these various projects some are such that they can only serve the purpose of providing water for irrigation. But there are those schemes also which besides irrigation, shall generate electricity, control floods and facilitate land navigation, etc.

Member: Which of them are the multi-purpose projects?

Mr. Gaurav: Projects like the Damodar Valley project, Bhakra Nangal Dam, Hirakud Dam, etc. are the most important multi-purpose projects.

Member: Do you know anything about the Damodar Valley Project?

Mr. Gaurav: This project is the biggest multi-purpose project in India. Its construction involved the building up of eight dams on the Damodar and a big barrage at Durgapur. Out of these dams seven serve as water storehouses. The aggregate controlled reservoir measures about 4,70,000 acre feet. The water is expected to irrigate over one million acres of hitherto barren land for all time to come and will also generate 1181 MW of power.

Member: What is the total power generating capacity of India's existing plants?

Mr. Gaurav: The total power generating capacity of our plants both, private and public—is about 100 GWH.

Member: Do you know where the National Metallurgical Laboratory and the Electro-Chemical Industries Research Laboratories are situated?

Mr. Gaurav: Sir, the former is situated at Jamshedpur and the latter at Karaikudi.

Member: What is the use of the Central Building Research Institute at Roorkee?

Mr. Gaurav: Now called the Roorkee University, it provides a nucleus for organised research on technical aspects of building material and methods. It helps to solve many problems of major importance to the country for which its advice is sought in its own field.

Member: Suppose the Government placed you in-charge of a big Housing Scheme, how would you proceed to make it as economical as possible?

Mr. Gaurav: Sir, I will very carefully analyse the whole scheme under the following heads:

1. The material and the labour required for it
2. Its architectural design
3. Its structural design; and then
4. I shall make a detailed programme of its works, administration and its execution.

I will undertake a personal examination of the site of the plan, and draw out with the help of expert draftsmen the whole plan of the buildings and lay down, according to the Government requirements, the minimum standards for plinths, heights and sizes of the rooms, the kinds of floors required, the areas of doors and windows and of the general standard of the buildings and the purpose for which they are required. Next I will call for tenders from experienced contractors who are known to have done this type of work, and select the one who ensures standard materials, skilled labour and a tender based on realistic estimation of costs. If the scheme is quite large, I will try to entrust the work to more than one contractor and bring about a healthy competition among them, always keeping a careful supervision over the whole work to see that everything is done according to programme and given specifications. I will also employ experienced men, preferably engineers, to keep watch over the whole scheme as it progresses so that no faulty or patch-work is done.

Chairman: You have mentioned in Bio-data, that you have acquaintance with volley-ball too besides cricket. Can you say what is the measurement of a Volley-ball ground?

Mr. Gaurav: The court or ground for volley-ball measures 60' × 30'.

Chairman: Can you tell us when Burma became independent?

Mr. Gaurav: Sir, Burma (now known as Myanmar) got her independence in 1948.

Chairman: Mr. Gaurav now please let us know what do you know about the 38th Parallel?

Mr. Gaurav: Sir, It is a demarcation line between North Korea and South Korea. When the Japanese surrendered and World War II drew to an end, it was decided by the Allied Powers that the North Zone of the 38th Parallel be occupied by the Soviet Union and the Southern part by the USA. This occupation was to be continued till circumstances would make it unnecessary. This later brought about the Korean war.

Chairman: Where is Hiroshima?

Mr. Gaurav: It is a place in Japan.

Chairman: What is it associated with?

Mr. Gaurav: It is that unfortunate city over which the first atom bomb was dropped in 1945 by a US aircraft.

Chairman: Where is the Hyde Park situated?

Mr. Gaurav: It is a part of old Abbey Park of Westminster and is a pleasure resort of London.

Chairman: And what is Kremlin?

Mr. Gaurav: It is the seat of the Russian Government in Moscow.

Chairman: Thank you, Mr. Gaurav, now you may go.

Mr. Gaurav: Thank you, Sir.

> ***Comments:*** *The candidate is intelligent and well-informed. He displays awareness regarding the latest developments. He is able to decide and the priorities with speed and accuracy and knows how to utilize the resources at his disposal to ensure optimum results.*

Model Interview-10

Mr. Rohan Rustogi is a B.E. and is called for the interview after passing the Indian Engineering Services Exam. He is a young and smart person with pleasant manners. He enters the room with a smile and greets the board members and the chairman.

The Interview

Mr. Rustogi: Good Morning, Sirs.

Board: Good Morning Mr. Rustogi, please take your seat.

Mr. Rustogi: Thank you sir (*after taking seat*).

Chairman: You are Mr. Rohan Rustogi?

Mr. Rustogi: Yes, Sir.

Chairman: When did you pass your B.E. ?

Mr. Rustogi: In 20..., Sir.

Chairman: What have you been doing since?

Mr. Rustogi: Sir, I am serving with Messrs Tata Iron & Steel as a Mechanical Engineering apprentice.

Chairman: What particular line do you want to join now?

Mr. Rustogi: I intend joining Mechanical Engineering, Sir.

Chairman: What methods of irrigation are in vogue in India?

Mr. Rustogi: In India we make use of wells, tanks, canals, tubewells, etc., to irrigate the land.

Chairman: How many kinds are there of canals?

Mr. Rustogi: Canals are of three kinds. One is the Inundation Canals; two, the Perennial Canals; and three, the Storage Canals.

Chairman: Can you tell us anything about the Bhakra Dam?

Mr. Rustogi: In the Bhakra Dam Project a dam has been laid across a gorge in the river Sutlej. It is one of the most important multi-purpose projects on which work has already been completed. It comprises a large dam 740 feet high across the gorge at Bhakra, which stores about 35 million acre feet of water and provides 6,600 cubic feet of water per second for a period of about nine months which is the dry part of the year.

The irrigation system commands an area of 45 million acres through 652 miles of lined canals and a network of distributaries. It generates 1200 million watts of power.

Chairman: Which Governmental body is responsible for the development of scientific research in India?

Mr. Rustogi: The Government of India has a Department of Science and Technology. This department is directly under the Prime Minister.

Chairman: Is there any other organisation carrying on research in the scientific field of knowledge?

Mr. Rustogi: Yes, Sir. There is the Council of Scientific and Industrial Research, established in 1942.

Chairman: On what other topics research work is being done in India?

Mr. Rustogi: We have numerous organisations carrying on research work in various spheres of scientific knowledge. There is, for example, the Bhaba Atomic Research Centre (BARC). Then there is the Indian Council of Agricultural Research, which encourages research in agriculture.

Member: What is a ballast?

Mr. Rustogi: It is the gravel, stone or other material placed in the hold of a ship to increase her stability when floating without cargo or with insufficient cargo.

Member: What is a bolometer?

Mr. Rustogi: It is an instrument for measuring radiant energy by determining the changes of resistance in an electrical conductor.

Member: And what is a control room?

Mr. Rustogi: It is a room used by the engineers of an electric power supply system for supervising the operation of the entire system.

Member: What does Sb stand for?

Mr. Rustogi: It is the symbol of antimony.

Member: Who invented the Powerloom?

Mr. Rustogi: Sir, it was Cartwright.

Member: Mr. Rustogi, in your application you have stated that you play football and volleyball. In what other games, besides these, are you interested?

Mr. Rustogi: Sir, I take interest in hockey and racing, too.

Member: What is the highest record in cricket?

Mr. Rustogi: It is 1107 runs in a match played between the Victoria vs New South Wales.

Member: What is the trophy associated with hockey?

Mr. Rustogi: Beighton Cup.

Member: What is the measurement of a football field?

Mr. Rustogi: Sir, its length is 100 yards to 130 yards; breadth 50 yards to 100 yards.

Member: What is the essential difference between a rocket and jet engine?

Mr. Rustogi: A rocket carries its own fuel and oxygen for combustion within it. In jet propulsion devices oxygen is obtained from the atmosphere.

Member: How is forward motion imparted in them?

Mr. Rustogi: They drive their forward thrust from the backward expulsion of a stream of liquid or gases.

Member: What sort of fuels are used in rockets and jet planes?

Mr. Rustogi: Explosive smokeless powder, cordite of liquids like alcohol, kerosene, gasoline. Both carry liquefied oxygen to support the combustion.

Member: What is the principle of motion on which these jets or rockets operate?

Mr. Rustogi: Newton's Third Law of Motion.

Member: What speed did the Russian Sputniks attain?

Mr. Rustogi: 17,000 miles per hour.

Chairman: What is the difference between neon and fluorescent lighting?

Mr. Rustogi: In neon lighting the neon gas is made to give a brilliant red orange glow by help of an electric charge when the gas is under low pressure. In fluorescent lighting, the gas in the lamp is Argon and a speck of mercury. The light in this form is white and is the result of the crystal fluorescing.

Chairman: Why is a parachute provided with a hole in the centre?

Mr. Rustogi: To impart stability to descent by allowing a small quantity of air to flow in and out. Without it the parachute will remain floating much longer than needed.

Chairman: How are clouds "seeded" to produce rain?

Mr. Rustogi: Dry ice or chemicals like tiny crystals of silver nitrate are scattered into rain clouds and the moisture is made to fall, thus creating artificial rain.

Chairman: Can you briefly trace the history of volleyball?

Mr. Rustogi: Yes, Sir, it was invented by William G. Morgan of USA in 1895. The original name, for reasons not known, given to the game was Miononette. In 1929 a United States Volleyball Trophy was declared and the International Open Trophy in 1945. This game is most popular in the United States of America. In India too, it is widely played.

Chairman: That's all, Mr. Rustogi.

Mr. Rustogi: Thank you Sir.

> **Comments:** *The candidate displays excellent awareness in various fields. He enjoys abundant common sense and self-confidence and meets all the challenges with determinations, tact and resourcefulness.*

Model Interview-11

Mr. Nandan is a handsome self-confident person who is called for an Engineering Services interview. He enters the room and greets the chairman along with members.

The Interview

Mr. Nandan: Good Morning, Sirs.

Chairman: Good Morning, Mr. Nandan. Please take your seat.

Mr. Nandan: Thank you Sir (*after taking seat*).

Chairman: What was your main subject in Engineering?

Mr. Nandan: Mechanical Engineering, Sir.

Chairman: Mr. Nandan, can you name some small-scale engineering industries that have grown-up in the country in recent years? Can you also tell us where they have grown up?

Mr. Nandan: Sir, among the recently-established engineering industries are those which manufacture textile accessories, such as pickers and bobbins. They are to be found in and around Kolkata. Other such industries are like those which manufacture bicycle components and accessories. They have grown up mostly in Punjab and West Bengal. In many parts of the country re-rolling mills and foundries have been established and those which produce binders, cutting machines, small presses, small spinning machines, iron casting, etc.

Chairman: Mr. Nandan as an engineer, you must be interested in the multi-purpose projects in India. Are you?

Mr. Nandan: Yes, Sir.

Chairman: Can you explain the Rihand Dam Project?

Candidate: This is one of the most important schemes completed by Uttar Pradesh. It comprised the construction of a masonry dam three hundred feet high, to impound water for about 14 lakh acres of land across the river Rihand in the Sonbhadra District.

Chairman: What is the approximate power generated by this dam?

Mr. Nandan: About 2.5 lakh KW.

Chairman: What is its effect on the irrigation of Uttar Pradesh?

Mr. Nandan: Sir, it has brought about 14 lakh acres of land under irrigation. This land had not been put to any use so far.

Member: What do you know about Tungabhadra Dam Project?

Mr. Nandan: This project is being executed by the Andhra and Karnataka Governments. It comprises the construction of a dam 162 feet high on the Tungabhadra river at Mallapuram. It will bring about 8.3 lakh acres of land under irrigation. The power generated will be about 22,500 KW.

Member: Now please tell us something about Nangal Dam Project.

Mr. Nandan: It is the joint venture of Punjab, Haryana and Rajasthan. It provided for a dam eight miles below the site of Bhakra Dam. The dam has diverted the river into the Nangal Hydro-Electric Canal for three power houses about 15 to 18 miles downstream the weir. The installed capacity of the three power houses is over 1200 million watts. It irrigates over 24 lakh hectares of land in the state of Punjab, Haryana and Rajasthan.

Member: Would you mind telling us something about the Chambal Valley Project?

Mr. Nandan: This project consists of three minor projects for the construction of dams on the Chambal river by the Rajasthan and Madhya Pradesh Governments. The main dam is about 200 ft. high.

Member: What will be the capacity of its water reservoir?

Mr. Nandan: The water reservoir is expected to accommodate 6.89 million acres of water. By tunnels about 14,00,000 acres can be irrigated from this reservoir.

Member: What will be the power generated from this project?

Mr. Nandan: About 2,10,000 KW.

Member: Suppose you are put in charge of a Government factory. What is the first thing you will do?

Mr. Nandan: The first thing I will do is to see the work which is being done there is not haphazard, for in a factory this results in enormous waste of time, energy, and material. In an engineering concern, for instance, a foreman may be handed the drawings and may be expected to produce the finished article. He is thus, made to arrange for everything the material, tools, extra machines if necessary and the requisite labour. And if he has to do all this in addition to his normal duties of supervision of work done in his department there are bound to be many mistakes and miscalculations.

Member: Yes, yes.

Mr. Nandan: May I give some definite example, Sir?

Member: Yes, by all means.

Mr. Nandan: For instance work might have been, in such shops, started on a job only to discover at a crucial stage that some material was lacking, or perhaps half the job is done when discovery is made that a mistake in the operation has prevented further progress. I will therefore, attach the first importance to the management of the factory on some well-planned basis.

Member: Well, then, what will be the basis of your planning?

Mr. Nandan: If I am given charge of the whole factory, I will create a separate production-planning department, leaving the foreman and workmen on the job they know best, *i.e.,* manufacturing the goods. In the planning department I will have specialists who would be made to work in close cooperation with one another. Next, I will arrange for complete work preparation before issuing instructions to the shops so that the workmen can concentrate on doing the job without wasting time looking for means and material with which to do it. I will also have a detailed scheduling of operations based on maximum plant utilisation.

Chairman: Yes, yes, go on if you have anything more to say.

Mr. Nandan: Sir, I will also have standardisation and simplification of all materials, tools and other elements and planned purchase of adequate material.

Chairman: Do you think you will be able to produce everything to schedule?

Mr. Nandan: Sir, what I have said represents an ideal state of affairs, in which everything runs like clockwork strictly according to plan. But there are always some snags, though engineers try to be as realistic as possible, still you cannot avoid the bottlenecks, and unforeseen difficulties. They are likely to disturb the time schedule based on an average uniform effort. This leaves a considerable margin for special efforts to overcome the hold-up, I have just now mentioned and this ensures that the overall plan proceeds smoothly, unruffled by any impediments.

Chairman: Mr. Nandan, you may go now.

Mr. Nandan: Thank you, Sirs.

> ***Comments:*** *The candidate is intelligent and well-informed. He displays awareness regarding the latest developments. He is able to decide the priorities with speed and accuracy and knows how to utilize the resources at his disposal to ensure optimum results.*

Model Interview for Bank Services: Probationary Officers

Model Interview-12

Mr. Gaffar Ansari is a resident of Bihar and is doing MA through correspondence after graduation in History (Hons) from Allahabad University, Allahabad. He believes in honest labour and has hobbies like educating adults, sports and reading newspapers. He concentrated on Bank PO exams. His hard labour has proved fruitful and he has been called for interview after qualifying the written test.

The Interview______________________________________

Gaffar : Good morning, Sir.

Chairman: Good morning. Take your seat, please. What is your name?

Gaffar : My name is Gaffar Ansari Sir.

Chairman : What is the name of your father?

Gaffar : The name of my father is Mohammed Idris, Sir.

Chairman: What is his occupation?

Gaffar : He works as an accountant in a private firm, Sir.

Chairman : What is the name of the firm and where is it situated?

Gaffar : Ansari Soap Works in Kolkata, Sir.

First Member: What is your educational qualification?

Gaffar: I passed my plus three examination in 2005, Sir.

First Member: How did you fare in the examination?

Gaffar: I secured 72.3% marks, Sir.

First Member: And marks in the Secondary Examination?

Gaffar: I got 59.3% marks in the Secondary Examination.

Second Member: What was the percentage of marks in English and Mathematics respectively in your Secondary Examination?

Gaffar: I secured 59.32% in English and 49% in Mathematics, sir:

Second Member: You were placed in the first division neither in Secondary Examination nor in the plus-two. Why?

Gaffar: I fell ill during my Secondary Examination and during the examination of Mathematics and Science papers,

I had high fever and headache. I could not get first division in my plus-two because I began the preparation only 3 months before the examination. The other reason for I could not concentrate was my mother's illness, Sir.

Chairman: You got very poor marks in Secondary and Senior Secondary, particularly in Mathematics. Will it not be difficult for you to pull on with the job?

Gaffar: It was only by chance that I fell ill on the day of Maths papers, which was my favourite subject, Sir. I'll not face any difficulty during my service period because of my poor marks in Maths. I can do my work soundly on the basis of my knowledge in that subject, Sir.

First Member: What subjects did you have in the plus two examination?

Gaffar : I had English, Economics, History, Urdu and Hindi as my combination.

First Member: Why is the year 1757 famous for?

Gaffar : The year 1757 is famous for Battle of Plassey, which was fought between the Nawab of Bengal and the English.

First Member: Who was the Nawab of Bengal then?

Gaffar : Sirajudaullah was the Nawab of Bengal.

Second Member: What is the year 1857 famous for?

Gaffar: 1857, is remembered as the year for India's First War of Independence. In 1857, Indian soldiers in the British Army revolted against the English.

Second Member: Who were the leading figures of the 1857 movement?

Gaffar: Mangal Pandey, Jhansi Ki Rani, Babu Kunwar Singh, Nana Saheb, Bahadur Shah Zafar, Hazrat Mahal, etc. were the leading figures in the revolt of 1857.

Chairman: Do you know about the Jallianwala Bagh episode? Where is it, and what is it famous for?

Gaffar: Jallianwala Bagh is in Amritsar in Punjab. It is famous for the Jallianwala Bagh Tragedy of 1919. The British

Police under the charge of Michael O' Dyer gunned down hundreds of Indians attending the meeting in the Jallianwala Bagh.

Second Member: Which important event do you associate, with the year 1942?

Gaffar: The year 1942 is associated with the Quit India Movement led by Indian National Congress. The Congress wanted the British to quit India.

Third Member: Do you have interest in sports?

Gaffar: Yes Sir. I have good interest in sports.

Third Member: How do you compare the Indian cricket team with the Australian team?

Gaffar: The Australian team is far better and stronger than the Indian team. At present Indian team is also performing well.

Chairman: How?

Gaffar: Recent records reveal its strength and position, sir.

First Member: In which company do you work at present, and since how long? .

Gaffar: I have been working in a clearing and forwarding agency for the last 6 months.

First Member: What is the nature of your work?

Gaffar : I am working in import department and my job is to debit the import licences, Sir.

First Member : How many copies of licences are there?

Gaffar: Two copies, namely, Customs Copy and Exchange Control Copy, Sir.

First Member: What nature of goods does your company clear?

Gaffar: We clear goods like organic and inorganic chemicals, varnishes, wallpapers, machinery items, dyestuffs, pigments, etc.

First Member: What are the currencies of Russia, USA. and UK?

Gaffar: Rouble, Dollar and Pound Sterling respectively, Sir.

Second Member: Is there anyone in the Banking Service in your family?

Gaffar: No, Sir. There is no one in Banking Service in my family.

Second Member: Would you not have got certain advantages if you had any relative in Banking services?

Gaffar: Excuse me, sir. I beg to differ with you. One's talent, way of thinking as well as style of working always differs from another's. In case one's father is in the Banking Service, one may be affected by hearing one's father talking about his work from very beginning. So, I think that there is no correlation between talent, way of thought and style of working.

Second Member: Why do you like to join the Banking service?

Gaffar: Banking sector is the significant service sector in India, so it will provide me opportunities to serve the people as well as my country.

Chairman: There are a large number of candidates seeking a job in the Banking sector, But there is a limited number of vacancies. How will you feel if you are not selected?

Gaffar: Excuse me, sir. I am sure to be one of successful candidates. I possess all the required eligibilities, *i.e.,* smartness, talent and, above all. I am very ambitious to attain success by dint of those qualities one can reach one's goal. So, I cannot rate myself below the successful candidates, Sir.

Second Member : Which State in India leads in tobacco production?

Gaffar: Andhra Pradesh, Sir.

Third Member: What is sericulture? And which state leads in sericulture?

Gaffar: The rearing of silk worms for silk production is called sericulture, Sir. Karnataka is the leading State in India in sericulture.

Third Member: Which day is observed as the Martyr's Day.

Gaffar: 30th January, the day the Father of the Nation, Mahatma Gandhi was assassinated in 1948.

Chairman: What is drip irrigation, and what are its benefits?

Gaffar: Sir, drip irrigation is the artificial application of water to the root zone of a plant drop by drop. Its benefits are saving excess of water, controlling weeds, minimising cost, saving time, saving extra cost of fertiliser and protecting land from alkalinity due to limited water supply.

Chairman: When is the International Yoga Day observed and since when?

Gaffar: Sir, It is observed on 21st June every year. It was first observed in 2015.

Chairman: Thank you Mr. Gaffar. You may go now.

Gaffar: Thank you, Sirs.

> **Comments:** *The candidate is fully acknowledged with his subject of study. Along with that, he is acquianted with latest development around him. He displays a confident personality with determination.*

Model Interview for Bank Services: Other Posts

Model Interview-13

Miss Anupama is a resident of Ranchi and a B.Sc. with Chemistry as Honours from Ranchi University. She has been a serious student throughout her career. She also has liking for Commerce. She believes in honest labour and has hobbies like educating adults and children. She has two year Diploma in Commercial & Secretarial Practice from Government Polytechnic for women, Ranchi. Her father is a good law practitioner. After B.Sc. Miss Anupama prepared seriously for Banking services. Her hard labour has proved fruitful and she has been called for interview after qualifying the written test.

The Interview

Anupama: May I come in, Sir?

Chairman: Yes, come in please.

Anupama: Good morning, Sirs.

Chairman: Good morning, please be seated.

Anupama: Thank you, Sir.

Chairman: Miss Anupama, what are your educational qualifications?

Anupama: Sir, I have done my B.Sc. with Chemistry as Honours from the Ranchi University and a two-year Diploma in Commercial & Secretarial Practice from Government Polytechnic for Women, Ranchi, I, topped in the State Board in this Diploma course.

First member: You've worked in an engineering concern as a stenographer, then as a stenographer in the Income Tax Office. Now you are a clerk in the New India Assurance Company, and all this within a year. What is the reason for such frequent changes?

Anupama : Sir, in the engineering concern the problem was the pay scale. They paid me less than the stipulated basic salary. In the Income Tax office, the work was routine; it was more bureaucratic red-tapism that is a hallmark of all government offices. I did not like the working conditions there.

Chairman: Do you know about the banking system?

Anupama: Yes Sir.

Chairman: What are the different types of cheques?

Anupama : Sir, we have, bearer, order, crossed, stale and postdated cheques commonly in use in the banking system.

Chairman: What is a post-dated cheque?

Anupama : Sir, a post-dated cheque is issued in advance, but it is honoured by the bank only on the date mentioned therein and not earlier.

First Member: What is a double entry system?

Anupama : Sir, it is a system of accounting which implies that every transaction has two aspects—debit and a corresponding credit.

Second Member: Miss Anupama, when we write the cash book, we make entries for receipt and payment of cash only. Isn't that a single entry system?

Anupama: No sir. When we enter any receipt or payment of cash in the cash book; there must be the other aspect of transaction of which cash has been received or paid and the entry for that aspect is made in the ledger account.

Chairman: How many commercial banks have been nationalised so far?

Anupama: Twenty, Sir.

Second Member: In which year was the Reserve Bank of India nationalised?

Anupama: I am sorry, I don't know the year, Sir.

Second Member: It was 1949. Now tell me the functions of the RBI.

Anupama : Sir, the Reserve Bank of India issues all paper currency except one-rupee notes. It acts as the Banker's Bank and also the Bank to the Government. It controls credit in order to avoid inflationary tendencies resulting from over expansion of credit.

Chairman: Who was Dr. APJ Abdul Kalam?

Anupama: He was an eminent scientist who later became the President of India between 2002 and 2007.

Chairman: Could you name one of his famous books?

Anupama: Yes, Sir. It is "India 2020–A Vision for the New Millennium".

Chairman: Who has been the only Indian lady to have been elected president of the UN General Assembly?

Anupama: Mrs. Vijayalakshmi Pandit, Sir. She died in December 1990.

Chairman: Miss Anupama, do you see movies?

Anupama: Yes Sir.

Chairman: Who is your favourite actress, and why?

Anupama: Sir, my favourite actress is Katrina Kaif because of her natural acting. She really lives the character she enacts.

Chairman: As a student of Chemistry Honours, which branch of the subject is special interest for you?

Anupama: Physical Chemistry, Sir.

Chairman: What is Physical Chemistry?

Anupama: This branch of Chemistry deals with theoretical principles, and is mainly concerned with the development of the theories and their applications to different systems.

First Member: Who was the first recipient of Nobel prize in Chemistry?

Anupama: Sir, it was Van Hoff.

First Member: What is a mechanical mixture?

Anupama: Sir, a mechanical mixture is a variety of matter which results when two or more substances are mixed together in any proportion, leading to any chemical combination. So, the component substances remain side by side, retaining their individual characteristic properties, such as gun powder which is a mechanical mixture of powdered sulphur, charcoal and nitre.

First Member: How does a law differ from a hypothesis?

Anupama: Sir, hypothesis may be just a tentative explanation or even speculation of an observation based on thoughts and imagination, without recourse to experimentation. On the other hand, law or generalised, principles are formulated after obtaining sufficient data about a given phenomenon by careful observation and critical study of the results of a series of well-planned experiments with sufficient refinement in methods and instrumentation.

First Member: Miss Anupama, please name the method by which a mixture of liquids having close boiling points can be separated?

Anupama: Sir, it is fractional distillation by which a mixture of liquids having different but close boiling points may be separated.

Second Member: What is a disproportionate reaction?

Anupama: Sir, it is a special type of reaction in which a compound decomposes into a lower valent and higher valent compound.

Second Member: What is the Greenhouse Effect?

Anupama: Sir, the amount of carbon dioxide in the air is gradually increasing with the rapid use of fuels like coal. Carbon dioxide absorbs a large fraction of earth's emitted radiation. Thus earth's emission is remitted into its surface. As a result, earth's surface is getting heated gradually. This is known as the Greenhouse Effect.

Second Member: What is TNT?

Anupama: Sir, TNT is tri nitro-toluene, which is a highly explosive organic compound. Second, TNT is a unit to measure the power of explosives.

Second Member: You've studied Physics upto degree level. What is S.I. unit of pressure?

Anupama: Sir, Bar is the unit of pressure in the S.I. System.

Third Member: Miss Anupama, now that you've answered a lot of questions about your specialized subject, would you tell me what is Blue Revolution?

Anupama: Sir, Blue Revolution means an increase in the production of fish.

Third Member: What is the colour behind you?

Anupama : White, Sir. (It was the colour of the wall of the room).

Third Member: What is psephology?

Anupama: Sir, it is the statistical analysis of election results.

Chairman: How would you feel if you are not selected in the interview?

Anupama: Sir, I would feel sorry for a moment but shall soon overcome the feeling. I strongly believe that perseverance and industry will enable me to attain my goal in life.

Chairman: Miss Anupama, the interview is over. You may go now.

Anupama: Thank you, Sirs.

> ***Comments:*** *The candidate is sincere and earnest in her approach and believes in hard work and systematic effort to achieve positive results. She has a cheerful and optimistic personality which will be useful in achieving goals.*

Model Interview for Railway Services

Model Interview-14

Mr. Rajesh Kumar is a candidate for the Interview of Indian Railway Service. He is postgraduate in History. He is a smart, good looking person full of energy and enthusiasm. When called for an interview he enters the room and greets all the members along with the Chairman.

The Interview

Mr. Rajesh: *(Comes gracefully with a smile on his face and says)* Good Morning to all of you Sirs.

Chairman: Good morning, take your seat.

Chairman : I see your application form that you have done your M.A. You could have chosen any other profession. What prompted you to opt for railway service?

Mr. Rajesh: Sir, I belong to the family of railway officers and as such I have developed an attitude and liking for a job in the railways. Moreover, if I am employed in railways, I will get plenty of opportunities to visit places of cultural and historical interest in India which is not so easy in other jobs.

Chairman: Does this mean you know a lot about the Indian Railways? Could you tell us when the first railway line was opened in India and in which part of the country?

Mr. Rajesh: Sir, first steam engine ran on 16 April, 1853. The first track, measuring 34km was laid between Bombay and Thana.

Member: What about other stations?

Mr. Rajesh: Sir, Calcutta was first linked to Delhi in 1860 and then the Calcutta-Bombay line was opened in 1870.

Member: To whom goes the credit of starting the railway system in India?

Mr. Rajesh: Sir, it was Lord Dalhousie, the then Governor-General of India who gets this credit.

Member: Which is the fastest train in India and on which route does it run?

Mr. Rajesh: Sir, India's fastest train is the Gatimaan Express. It runs between New Delhi and Agra, and was introduced in 2016. It has a speed of 160 km/hour and covers a distance of 188 km in 100 minutes.

Chairman: Who is responsible for the administration and management of Indian Railway?

Mr. Rajesh: Sir, the responsibility for the administration and management of railways is with the Railway Board which is under overall supervision of a Cabinet Minister assisted by a minister of state. The Board consists of chairman who is an ex-officio secretary to the Government in the Ministry of Railways, Financial commissioner and four other members who are all ex-officio Secretaries to the Government.

Chairman: What is the status of the Indian Railways in the world?

Mr. Rajesh: Sir, the Indian Railways has grown into Asia's largest and the world's second largest railway system after USA. It is also the world's largest employer. That is not all, India has the longest railway platform in the world at Gorakhpur in U.P. which measures 1355.4 metre in length.

Chairman: When was the first electric train introduced in India?

Mr. Rajesh: Sir, in 1925 when Victoria Terminus and Kurla rail route was electrified.

Chairman: Is there any train service between India and Pakistan? If so what is the name of the train?

Mr. Rajesh: Yes, Sir, there is regular train service between India and Pakistan. The name of the train is Samjhauta Express, the name given to it in 1971 after the Shimla Accord.

Member: Name the train that covers the longest route.

Mr. Rajesh: Sir, it is Vivek Express running between Kanyakumari and Dibrugarh and covers a distance 4286 km.

Chairman: Is there a compensation for the railway employee injured in an accident while on duty?

Mr. Rajesh: Yes, Sir, from July 1990 the Ministry of Railway enforced a new Railway Act, replacing the act of 1890. Under this act an employee injured in an accident while on duty will be given the same compensation as a passenger. The liability of the Railways for death and injuries in an accident has been enhanced under the new Act with the next of kin of the dead passenger or employee being entitled to maximum compensation of ₹ 20 lakh.

Member: Where is the rail coach factory located?

Mr. Rajesh: Sir, it is at Kapurthala in Punjab.

Chairman: We think this will be enough. You may go now, please.

Mr. Rajesh: Thank you, Sirs.

> ***Comments:*** *The candidate is well-informed about the latest developments. He is methodical and systematic in planning and organising task and their implementation. He is very rational regarding issues of national importance.*

Model Interview-15

Mr. Rohan Ranjan, a candidate full of self-confidence and energy, is called to the interview room. He enters the room silently and offers his salutations to the Chairman and the members of the Board.

The Interview

Chairman: Good morning Mr. Rajan, have your seat please.

Mr. Rajan: Thank you, Sir.

Chairman: Mr. Rajan, where do you come from?

Mr. Rajan: From Uttar Pradesh, Sir.

Chairman: I found that your main subject was Economics both in your B.A. and in M.A. You secured a third division in B.A. and a first division in M.A. How do you account for it?

Mr. Rajan: When I was in B.A. I did not devote sufficient time and attention to my studies. Instead I was fully occupied with the college union activities. I was the General Secretary of the College Union and was responsible for arranging and organising a number of activities. In my M.A. Final I did not contest any union election and this automatically helped me to devote more attention to my studies.

Chairman: Mr. Rajan why do you want to opt for the Indian Railway Service after the training?

Mr. Rajan: Only due to my interest and liking Sir.

First Member: I find that you had Education as one of your subjects in B.A. Why did you not go for the teaching profession?

Mr. Rajan: Sir, undoubtedly teaching is a noble profession, but at present the emoluments offered to teachers are comparatively very low and one cannot remain satisfied with leading a noble profession when one finds it difficult to make both ends meet.

Chairman: I am afraid, Mr. Rajan the pay scales of Degree Colleges compete favourably with any other Civil Services. What have you to say?

Mr. Rajan: Sir, you are right. Now the pay scales have been revised. But there is no chance for promotion in an affiliated college. You start and finish in the same cadre. This leads to dissatisfaction.

First Member: Is money everything in this world, Mr. Rajan?

Mr. Rajan: Money may not be everything, Sir, but in the present economic conditions one cannot lead a happy life without sufficient money.

Second Member: Why is the Railway Budget presented separately and not as a part of the general budget?

Mr. Rajan: Sir, the Railways are the largest single nationalised industry of our country. The Railway revenues are subject to large scale fluctuations. It was, therefore, thought desirable to have the railway budget separated from the general budget.

Second Member: Do the railways make any contribution to the general revenue?

Mr. Rajan: Yes Sir. the Railways do. As far as I think the rate of contribution is about 6%.

Chairman: How many kilometres do the Indian Railways cover?

Mr. Rajan: Sir, the Indian Railways cover a route of over sixty thousand kilometres. The Indian Railways system is the second largest network in the world.

Chairman: Do you have any idea of the number of people travelling daily by the Indian Railways?

Mr. Rajan: Sir, it is difficult to give an exact idea but I think about one crore passengers travel every day by the Indian Railways.

Chairman: Have you any idea of the number of people who travel without ticket?

Mr. Rajan: Sir, studies made in this respect show that about 6 to 7 per cent of the passengers travel ticketless.

Chairman: How much loss do the railways suffer on this account?

Mr. Rajan: Sir, it is between ₹ 30 to 35 crore annually.

Chairman: What steps have the Railway authorities taken to check ticketless travelling?

Mr. Rajan: In order to check ticketless travelling surprise checks are made on a large scale. The ticket checking staff is supported by contingents of Railway Police. Heavy penalties are imposed on ticketless passengers. The checking staff is accompanied by Railway magistrates who try the cases on the spot. Those who fail to pay the fine are sent to jail.

Chairman: When were the Indian Railways nationalized?

Mr. Rajan: They were nationalized after India became independent. Before independence the Indian Railways were run by private companies like the East India Railway Company.

Chairman: When was the Railway Industry nationalized in England?

Mr. Rajan: Sir, the Railways in England were nationalized in 1945 when the Government of Labour Party came into power.

First Member: How many different types of gauges are there in the Indian Railways?

Mr. Rajan: There are three types of gauges—broad gauge, metre gauge and narrow gauge.

First Member: Can you name some of the narrow gauge Railways?

Mr. Rajan: Sir, there are very few narrow gauge railway lines in India. One narrow gauge railway line runs from Siliguri to Darjeeling. Another runs from Kalka to Simla.

First Member: What is the central objective of the Five Year Plan?

Mr. Rajan: It is to carry India forward on the path of development. The strategy will be adopted to ensure 10% annual growth-rate of the economy so as to realize the dream of a developed country by 2020.

First Member: What was the growth-rate in the 10th Five Year Plan?

Mr. Rajan: It was around 8% Sir.

Chairman: Can you name some present women tennis stars of world repute?

Mr. Rajan: Venus Williams, Serena Williams, Justine Henin, Maria Sharapova, Amelie Mauresmo at the top of the tennis world.

Chairman: Name the two top stars of Tennis in India.

Mr. Rajan: Leander Paes and Mahesh Bhoopati Sir.

Chairman: Who is India's woman tennis star?

Mr. Rajan: Sania Mirza Sir.

Chairman: Now you may go Mr. Rajan.

Mr. Rajan: Thank you, Sir.

> ***Comments:*** *The candidate has excellent understanding of current national and international events and trends. He is aware of latest developments in this field and there is sound logic and reasoning in his arguments.*

Model Interview for Income Tax Inspector

Model Interview-16

Mr. Suradip Chakraborty is a resident of Orissa. He has been a bright student since his school days. He has always scored good marks during his academic career. He has graduated in Zoology (Hons) with 71 per cent marks. He believes in hard labour. He has been finally selected in SSC Graduate Level Exam 20...–Scheme A for the post of Inspector of Income Tax.

The Interview____

Suradip: May I come in, Sir?

Chairman: Yes, come in, Please take your seat. (*He greet them all and takes his seat and makes himself comfortable*)

Chairman: What is your name?

Suradip: Sir, My name is Suradip Chakraborty.

Chairman: What is your educational qualification?

Suradip: Sir, I have completed my graduation in Zoology Honours with first division in the year 20.... I have also completed Advance Diploma in computer Software in 20....

Chairman: Well, then what have you been doing since you completed your studies?

Suradip: Sir, after completion of my studies I have been preparing for various competitive exams like SSC, Banks, Railways etc.

First Member: What is the zoological name of Giraffe?

Suradip: Sorry madam, I don't know.

First Member: O.K. Then, what is the zoological name of frog?

Suradip: Madam, the zoological name of frog is Rana tigrina.

First Member: What do you mean by herbivorous, carnivorous and omnivorous animals?

Suradip: Madam, the animals which feed on plants are called herbivorous, the animals which feed on flesh of other animals are called carnivorous and the animals which feed on both plants and animals are called omnivorous animals.

First Member: Which is the largest phylum in the animal kingdom?

Suradip: Madam, it is the Arthropoda phylum.

Chairman: How many times have you dissected frog?

Suradip: Sir, I have dissected frog many times during the practical classes.

Chairman: Can you explain me the process of dissection of frog?

(Suradip explains accordingly).

Chairman: You have completed Advanced Diploma in Computer Software. Then what do you mean by software?

Suradip: Sir, software means the programmes of the computer.

Second Member: You have won many prizes in essay writing, debate, quiz competitions at the district level. Can you tell me any one topic of your essay competition and the summary to that essay?

(Suradip replies in detail accordingly).

Second Member: Draw the map of Odisha and locate your district there?

(Paper and pencil are given to Suradip. He draws the map of Odisha and locates his district Kalahandi there).

Third Member: What is your view on reservation policy in government jobs?

Suradip: Sir, Indian society is divided on the basis of castes over the ages. Lower caste people are still discriminated today. Reservation is a step in the right direction to bring equality in the society. But it should be implemented in the true sense of serving the purpose.

Third Member: When was the state of Odisha created?

Suradip: Sir, Odisha was create on 1st April, 1936 out of Bihar state.

Third Member: What is your view on mass agitation against industrialisation in Odisha?

Suradip: Odisha is an economically backward state. Only industrialisation will bring it to the mainstream. The mass agitation is only due to improper rehabilitation policy adopted by the companies. So proper rehabilitation of the displaced people and providing employment opportunities to local inhabitants will solve the problem to a great extent.

Third Member: What are the important news of today?

Suradip: Sir, the important news of today are: India has successfully launched another satellite in space, UN General Secretary has lauded the role of India in world peace, and India has won the World Cup in Cricket.

Chairman: Thank you Mr. Suradip. You may go now.

(Suradip thanks all of them and leaves the room)

> ***Comments:*** *The candidate is fully acknowledged with his subject of study. Along with that, he is acquianted with latest development around him. He displays a confident personality with determination.*

Model Interview for Custom Inspector

Model Interview-17

Mr. Pradip Kumar has been finally selected for the post of Inspector Examiner in the department of customs. He appeared in the SSC combined Main (Graduate Level) exam. 20... scheme A for the posts of (a) SI in CBI/Inspector (Central Excise/ Preventive officer/Examiner).

The Interview____

Pradip: May I come in, Sir?

Chairman: Yes, do come in.

Pradip: Good afternoon to all of you, Sirs.

Chairman: Good afternoon. Please take your seat.

Pradip: Thank you, Sir.

First Member: Your name, please.

Pradip: My name is Pradip Kumar, Sir.

First Member: O.K. Mr. Kumar, you have done graduation in Chemistry Honours. Haven't you?

Pradip: Yes, Sir.

First Member: Mr. Kumar, your details indicate that you are presently associated with All India Radio.

Pradip: Yes Sir, I am employed as upper division clerk in the office of Directorate General, All India Radio, New Delhi.

Chainman: Mr. Kumar, it is good that you are not an unemployed. It seems, you oriented yourself to get a job as early as possible after your graduation.

Pradip: Yes, Sir. I belong to a middle class family. I like to share the responsibilities of my family with my parents. It gives me satisfaction.

Chairman: It's all right, Mr. Kumar. Please tell me when did radio broadcast start in India? Please inform me about its journey to Akashvani.

Pradip: Sir, radio broadcasts started in India in 1923 when the first programme was broadcast by the Radio club of Bombay. This was followed by two privately owned transmitters at Bombay and Calcutta. The Government of India took them over in 1927 and started operating them under the name of Indian Broadcasting service. In 1936, the name of the service was changed to All India Radio. Since 1957, it is known as Akashvani.

Chairman: What is Yuva Vani?

Pradip : It is an important service of the AIR which gives programmes for the youth from nearly 75 stations. This service provides a forum for the youth to present their viewpoint by participating in talks discussions, interviews, plays, features and music. It is a service of the youth, by the youth and for youth.

Chairman: You have collected a good information, Mr. Pradip. It encourages me to know a little more. What is Prasar Bharti?

Pradip: Thank you, Sir, for your compliments. Sir, All India Radio and Doordarshan functioned under the Ministry of Information as two separate departments before November 1997 when the Government of India decided to place them under an autonomous broadcasting corporation of India known as Prasar Bharti. It determines the broadcast policy and has full control over programmes.

Second Member: Mr. Kumar, you are a graduate in Chemistry. What is a base in chemistry?

Pradip: Sir, bases are substances which contain hydroxyl group and form hydroxyl ions in solution. According to Bronsted Lowry concept, bases are those substances which accept protons.

Second Member: What do you mean by colloids?

Pradip: The substances like starch, gum, glue etc. which are non-crystalline and in dissolved state do not diffuse or have a little tendency to pass through the animal or vegetable membrane are called colloids.

Second Member: What is an alloy?

Pradip: It is a homogeneous mixture of two or more metals which looks like a single metal.

Second Member: What do you mean by dry ice?

Pradip: Dry ice is solid carbon dioxide. It is prepared by suddenly releasing the pressure of liquid carbon dioxide under a pressure of 58 atmospheres. The carbon dioxide falls in the form of snow and is compressed at a pressure of 2000 lbs per square inch to give dry ice.

Second Member: What is the difference between cast iron and wrought iron?

Pradip: Cast iron, also called pig iron, contains 2.5-4.5% carbon and is brittle. It cannot be hammered and does not rust easily. It is used in making certain tools. Wrought iron contains. 0.1-0.25% carbon only and is soft. It is used in making fine parts and electromagnets.

Second Member: What is the difference between caustic soda, washing soda and baking soda?

Pradip: Sir, caustic soda is sodium hydroxide and is a very strong base. It is hygroscopic and very corrosive. Washing soda is sodium carbonate which is a weaker base. It is a basic salt in nature and is less hygroscopic. It is much less corrosive. Baking soda is sodium bicarbonate. It is a very mild base and non-corrosive.

Third Member: Mr. Kumar, when do we observe International Women's Day?

Pradip: On March 8, Sir.

Third Member: What is the difference between slaked lime and quick lime?

Pradip: Quick lime (CaO) is a basic oxide of calcium which on treatment with water forms calcium hydroxide with the evolution of large amounts of heat. Calcium hydroxide [Ca(OH)$_2$] is known as slaked lime. Quick lime (as CaO) is used in metallurgical processes whereas slaked lime is used for white washing buildings etc.

Third Member: What do you mean by LSD?

Pradip: LSD stands for lysergic acid diethyl amide. It is a synthetic material which, when taken, causes hallucinations. It is classified under the term narcotic.

Third Member: Which political scientist has said: Power tends to corrupt and absolute power corrupts absolutely?

Pradip: Lord Acton, Sir.

Chairman: Thank you Mr. Pradip. The interview is over. You may go now. Have a nice day.

Pradip: Thank you all, Sirs.

> ***Comments:*** *The candidate is intelligent and well-informed. He displays awareness regarding the latest developments. He is able to decide the priorities with speed and accuracy and knows how to utilize the resources at his disposal to ensure optimum results.*

Model Interview for Judicial Services

Model Interview-18

Prem Nath Ahuja is a young man of medium height and lean build, appearing for the Judicial Services personality test.

The Interview

Ahuja: (*With a pleasant smile on his lips and radiating warmth and interest in his eyes, he looks up to the Chairman and Members and proceeds to greet them.*)

Good morning to you all, Sirs. (*He continues to remain in attention position awaiting the response from the Board*).

3rd Member (*A retired General from the Army*): (*Observing and appreciating the correct and smart way in which the* *candidate has been standing at attention position*) At ease, Mr. Ahuja, your records do not show that you underwent any NCC or other military training. Nevertheless, you seem to have had fairly good exposure to it. How did you manage it?

Ahuja: (*Obeying the orders and changing to 'at ease' position*) Thank you, Sir. My training is rather informal and a byproduct of my sports activities. I was an active and keen sportsman both at school and college and the sportsmen are also required to do the march past. Thus one of the instructors from NCC taught us the foot drill.

3rd Member: This is very good. By the way, please be seated.

Ahuja: Thank you, Sir. *(He sits down smartly without any unnecessary movements. The 3rd Member continues with his questions).*

3rd Member: You have indicated that your hobby is amateur dramas. How could you find time for dramatic activities when you are tied up with sports all the time?

Ahuja: We have the rehearsals, mostly at night. This suits the other members of our local dramatic club also as most of them are office-goers. In any case, I act only in two or three dramas in a year.

3rd Member: Can you give some more details about your hobby, I mean what roles you play in the dramas? Where and by whom they are organised and put on board? Who finances them? Do you follow my questions?

Ahuja: (*With a pleasant smile*) We have a recreation club in our locality, Sir, and it has a dramatic wing along with other club activities like tennis, swimming, library, etc. At the moment I happen to be the secretary of the dramatic set-up. The club provides some funds and bulk of the expenses are met through sale of tickets when we stage the dramas. We also bring out a brochure on the occasion of staging a play and the advertisements in the brochure are another source of revenue.

The members of the dramatic wing also pay a nominal monthly subscription.

3rd Member: What is the most expensive item in staging an amateur drama?

Ahuja: I would say the rent we have to pay for the hall which incidentally includes electricity, furniture, etc. If it is a historical play, the costumes, settings, etc. may also turn out to be expensive.

3rd Member: In your experience, what is the most difficult thing in organising an amateur drama?

Ahuja: *(Smiles)* Looking back nothing seems to be easy. But two things are really difficult. The first is the sale of tickets for the drama. The cooperation of the lady members is most essential for this purpose. The second, I would say, is organising the rehearsals. It involves so much work, coordination and cooperation of everybody.

2nd Member: *(Who intervenes at this stage)* Well, don't you think that the dramas are rather outdated in these days of colour TV and films?

Ahuja: *(Smiling)* I do agree with you, Sir, that TV and films have certain advantages. But dramas have their own appeal. You find dramas subtly incorporated in TV as well as in the cinema. Secondly, for those who are interested in a hobby, the amateur drama provides an excellent outlet. Those engaged in professional theatre know how to fight the cinema and TV and ensure their survival. Even in advanced countries, where TV, film and video are far more in vogue, the theatre is holding its own place. Hence, I won't say that dramas are outdated, either as a business or as a pastime.

In fact, theatre has been a stepping stone for many a film celebrity like Prithviraj Kapur, Raj Kapur, Prem Nath of Prithvi Theatres, etc. Anupam Kher, the former President of Film Censor Board, is a product of National School of Drama, New Delhi. The same is true of Naseeruddin Shah, Irrfan Khan, Raj Pal Yadav and many more.

Ramleelas held every year are visual theatrical depiction of the epic Ramayana. Theatres are thus the source for search of talent for films and TV. Both can co-exist, though of late, TV has overtaken both films and theatre.

Chairman: I am ready to concede your point that the theatre could still be relevant despite the growing dominance of TV and cinema. However, I am sure you should have done better in your studies or for that matter, even in sports if you had directed your time and energy towards them instead of dramas. Do you agree?

Ahuja: *(Smiling pleasantly)* Well, Sir, with your kind permission I agree to disagree. We all know that all work and no play makes Jack a dull boy. We do need diversions and hobbies so that we can have rest and relaxation after which we can tackle the assigned work more vigorously. I have not done badly either in studies or in sports. Certainly, there is room for improvement and it will be my endeavour to do better and excel. But I would like to submit that involvement in my hobby helps me to do better. It is a help and not hindrance, Sir. In any case, that is my personal experience.

Chairman: What do you think of Indian film censorship? How could you reconcile it with the freedom of expression as a Fundamental Right guaranteed by the Constitution?

Ahuja: Cinema is a powerful medium which has a great appeal and ready accessibility to the masses. Cinema influences the conduct and behaviour of our youth in a very big way. Hence, we should not permit the abuse of cinema in India. The film industry is mainly interested in making profits by any means. It has yet to evolve a code of conduct and apply self-restraint.

In fact, cinema is openly flouting our cultural values and ethos and infusing lurid Western civilisation in dress, manners, social intercourse, and in glorification of crime, etc. The most harmful inroad it has made is with regard to advocacy for permissive society, nudity of women, etc. Even the North-East militant groups have threatened that they won't permit screening films. It is no secret that many of crime incidents draw their inspiration from films. It is, therefore, high time that the Film Censor Board fully enforces a code of conduct reflecting true Indian culture. As regards freedom of expression, it is subject to public order, decency and morality. Such licentious freedom is against the national interest.

4th Member: How the independence of the judiciary in India is being ensured? Would you say it is functioning with independence as it should be?

Ahuja: To a great extent, the independence of the judiciary is safeguarded by the Constitution itself. For instance, the pay, etc. of the judges cannot be reduced. Once appointed, the judges cannot be removed except through impeachment by Parliament and they can serve till they attain the age of retirement. But the executive has some say in the appointment of the judges to the Supreme Court and the High Courts. Similarly, the executive has some leverage in the appointment of the Chief Justices. With a view to reducing political influence, it has also been enacted that one-third of the judges of each State High Court should be from outside the State. With a view to reducing the bureaucratic and political interference in the appointment of judges, the formation of a judicial commission has been envisaged. However, the independence of the judge depends by and large on himself only. He could be independent to the extent he chooses to be.

4th Member : Would you say that the independence of the judiciary is vital for the survival and growth of democracy?

Ahuja: *(Smiles)* Well, Sir, there cannot be two opinions that judicial independence is really essential for survival of democracy. Whenever the Fundamental Rights of an individual are threatened, he can approach the courts for the safeguard of the same. If there are no courts, who would rectify the wrong done to him? Courts are guardians of the Constitution which is the backbone of democracy. In India, as in England, the

Parliament is supreme and the judiciary cannot set aside any law passed by the legislature except when it infringes the basic structure of the Constitution.

4th Member: Do you not think that in our country, judiciary has not enjoyed the same status as it is doing in the United Kingdom?

Ahuja: Yes Sir, I agree with you. Despite supremacy of the Parliament, the judiciary in the United Kingdom is enjoying real independence as compared to India. The British tradition, public opinion, free Press, etc. ensure that each organ of the government plays its assigned role without interfering in the jurisdiction of others. Thus, for the growth and survival of democracy, I agree, judicial independence which accepts and respects the independence of the legislature and executive and also the electorate, is essential.

5th Member: What would have been Israel's reaction, if the Iranian Opposition candidate Mr. Mir Hossein Mousavi had succeeded in defeating Mr. Ahmadinejad in the Iranian presidential election on June 12, 20...?

Ahuja: The win of Mr. Mousavi would not have been in the interest of Israel. The head of Israel's Mossad, Mr. Meir Degan has been reported to have said recently that Mr. Mousavi's win would have spelled big problems for Israel. In fact, it was taken as a subtle acknowledgement of political realities in Teheran. This view was expressed by Mr. Degan in course of his meeting with the Foreign Affairs and Defence Committee of Knesset *i.e.*, parliament on June 16, 20... .

5th Member: What did he actually mean by such a statement?

Ahuja: The fact is that the Israeli spymaster was able to foresee that the protests in Iran would run out of steam. He meant to say that election fraud in Iran is not different from what happens in liberal states during elections. The struggle over the election results in Iran is internal and is unconnected to its strategic aspirations including Iran's nuclear programme. His explanation was this that the world already knew Mr. Ahmadinejad. Had the reformist candidate Mousavi won, Israel must have had a more serious problem, because it would have had the urgency of explaining to the world the danger of the Iranian threat, because Mr. Mousavi is perceived in the international arena as a moderate element. We should not forget that Iran's nuclear programme was commenced when Mr. Mousavi was the Iranian Prime Minister.

5th Member: Do you think Mr. Dagan's views were correct?

Ahuja : Yes, Sir. His assessment was faultless. In fact, the regime's base has benefited from Ahmadinejad's largesse and the rest of Iranian society is not sure whether anyone could do better. Today, he is the authentic leader of the Khomeinist movement. Mr. Mousavi or former President Mr. Khatami or for that matter any other prominent figure, cannot match his feat.

5th Member: Do you feel that the induction of all-out industrialisation linked to high technology and computers would be able to resolve the problem of poverty in India?

Ahuja: Sir, heavy industry linked to high technology and computers may not be able to help eradicate poverty in the country, particularly at this juncture where we also have to cope up with other problems like unemployment, illiteracy and population explosion. Even in America, Germany and Japan there are rich and poor people. These countries also have the problem of unemployment. They are now greatly worried about economic recession. They depend on export to other countries of their technology and manufactured goods and they want raw materials at cheap cost from underdeveloped and developing countries. Similarly, China, despite its Communism and state-controlled economy, has not been able to overcome poverty and unemployment. I will, therefore, recommend rural development through well-knit infrastructure and establishment of small scale and village industries instead of committing our resources on heavy industries since it takes a long gestation period for the capital intensive heavy industries, to produce results.

5th Member: Do you want to suggest that industralisation is less important than the growth of small scale industries?

Ahuja: No Sir, not at all. Industrialisation is as much important as the growth of small scale industries. But, Sir, permit me to add that I am not against industrialisation. The difference of view is only on timing and emphasis. For poverty alleviation, we have to check our rapid population growth through suitable incentives as also disincentives.

6th Member: What, according to you, is the basic thrust and rationale of the Budget 20...-... ?

Ahuja: Sir, in its essential thrust the Budget tries to address the abrupt termination of what was described by the previous Finance Minister as the absorbing and exciting Indian growth story. By and large, it is found that global economic, financial, social and systemic crises have reached India, by way of forcing a slowdown of the Indian economy's hyper growth. It is not recognised that the poor are faced with exclusion even when the market forces-led status quo growth marches ahead vigorously and the going gets really tough for these marginally included sections when the drivers of growth-wagon suffer bouts of recession. Therefore, tailormade task for any manager of a liberalised economy is to restore the high growth rate era as early as it is possible.

6th Member: Do you think the Budget promises anything new compared to earlier Budgets?

Ahuja: To my mind, the Budget has been prepared keeping in view the fact that the slowdown has been witnessed in India prior to the global slowdown. I mean, particularly, in the manufacturing sector. The slowdown was witnessed even in the face of about 30 per cent investment growth in this sector. Thus the global slowdown came at a time when the inner contradictions flowing from the neglect of the home market, qualitative and structural aspects of growth process capable of responding to the indigenous conditions and compulsions were already making their presence felt.

6th Member: Why do you think so?

Ahuja: I have arrived at this conclusion because of the move towards a somewhat more liberal spending by the Union Government on social programmes. Though it is not very sizeable compared to the customary spending on infrastructure for the elites and the affluent section's other public and quasi-public goods and services. It seems capable of combining in the short term, the pursuit of the narrow economic agenda with a little broader social agenda. If this is what has been done, one may say that a process of reconciling conflicting pulls and pressures has been initiated. This had not been witnessed for quite some time and is altogether new.

5th Member: Why did the Opposition express its annoyance over the joint statement that came out of the meeting between the Indian and Pakistani Prime Ministers in Sharm-el-Sheikh in July 20... ?

Ahuja: The Opposition was, in fact, opposed to one sentence in the statement, which read "Pak Prime Minister mentioned that Pakistan has some information on threats in Balochistan and other areas." Otherwise the statement is all right. In principle, as common perception goes, the two countries can restart talks on issues relating to Kashmir, demilitarisation and water resources. Both countries acknowledged that terrorism was the major threat they faced and agreed to share real time intelligence on terrorist threats. The Pakistani Prime Minister pledged to bring perpetrators of the Mumbai attacks to justice at the earliest. He also handed over a 36-page dossier on the action Islamabad had taken to bring those behind the attacks to justice.

6th Member: Do you think, the criticism of the non-Left opposition parties and the Congress party's lukewarm reception to the joint statement will hinder the dialogue process?

Ahuja: Yes Sir. It is obvious that all that has taken place does not bode well for an early resumption of the dialogue process. Senior Congress functionaries also criticised Dr. Manmohan Singh for agreeing to sign on the statement, although the Congress formally supported his statement in Parliament. On the other hand, back home, the Pakistani Prime Minister said that a dossier on Indian involvement had been presented to the Indian Prime Minister at Sharm-el-Shaikh. This is really unfortunate. Unless the peace process moves forward, there are indications that the Pakistan Army will remain stationed on its eastern borders.

4th Member: What forced the Pakistani President to skip the NAM Summit and dispatch his Prime Minister instead?

Ahuja: Dr. Manmohan Singh had usually adopted a militant posture since his first official interaction with then Pakistani President Mr. Asif Ali Zardari, on the sidelines of the Shanghai Cooperation Organisation (SCO) Summit in Yekaterinburg. In Yekaterinburg, Russia in June 20..., Mr. Singh brusquely expressed before the assembled media his approach towards Pakistan. He clearly stated that he had a one-point programme and it was to ensure that Islamabad stopped its soil being used for terrorism in India. Mr. Zardari felt embarrassed and could not feel at ease with the Indian Prime Minister issuing diktats in front of the media. That is why, it is said, he skipped the NAM Summit and sent his Prime Minister instead.

4th Member: Then what was the cause of the sudden change of attitude?

Ahuja: Sir, I think the sudden change of attitude on the Indian side with regard to starting the dialogue must be behind the-scenes diplomatic pressure from the United States. I feel so because the joint statement came just before the visit of the then US Secretary of State Ms. Hillary Clinton. Top US administration already see the Kashmir problem having some connection with the Afghanistan-Pakistan issue.

Chairman: In your bio data, you have mentioned that you would like to travel. Let's suppose you get the choice to visit a foreign country of your choice. Which country would you like to visit and why?

Ahuja: I shall opt for Japan, Sir. It is comparatively a small-sized country with high population density. It has hardly any natural resources to boast of. It also suffered the worst defeat in World War II and two of its large cities, Hiroshima and Nagasaki, were wiped out by atomic bombs. After the war it was occupied by the US army and even today it depends to a very large extent on the US support for its external security. Yet within a few decades, it not only regained its industrial capacity but today it has surpassed even America in the automobile and electronic spheres. The Japanese miracle is a tribute to its people and their culture. Hence, I feel I can learn a lot by visiting Japan. As regards sight-seeing, Japan has a lot to offer. Hiroshima and Nagasaki are flourishing cities today.

> ***Comments:*** *In brief, this smart and well-dressed candidate has shown himself as intelligent and imaginative person who could perceive things in their true perspective. His grasp is excellent and he enjoys a wealth of ideas. He present his views with conviction, authority and eloquence to sway his listeners and create a strong, favourable and lasting impact on them. His boldness, pragmatic approach and dynamism coupled with sterling qualities of character like loyalty, sincerity and integrity enable him to establish himself as the favourite candidate and natural winner.*

Model Interview for Airforce Services

Model Interview-19

Mr. Raman enters the interview room with a pleasant smile and confident manner.

The Interview

Mr. Raman: Good Morning, Sirs.

Chairman: Good Morning Mr. Raman, please take your seat.

Mr. Raman: Thank you sir (after taking his seat).

Chairman: What do you mean by air-borne forces?

Mr. Raman: Sir, these are troops carried in an aeroplane or glider, and usually dropped by parachute behind enemy lines, or in the immediate vicinity of some particular target.

Chairman: Do you know what ATC stands for?

Mr. Raman: This abbreviation stands for Air Training Corps. This was established in England in 1941 in order to prepare Britain's youth for Air Service in the RAF or in the Fleet Air Arm.

Chairman: And what is ATA?

Mr. Raman: This stands for Air Transport Auxiliary. This is a civilian organisation formed in England at the outbreak of the Second World War for delivering aircraft from the factories to RAF and Fleet Air Arm.

Chairman: What is your favourite game, Mr. Raman.

Mr. Raman: I play football, Sir.

Chairman: What is a free kick?

Mr. Raman: In the event of any infringement or of a player being sent off the field, a free kick is awarded to the opposite side from the place where the infringement occurred.

Chairman: How many types of free kicks are there?

Mr. Raman: Free kicks are of two types: (*i*) Direct from which a goal can be scored against the offending side, and (*ii*) Indirect from which a goal cannot be scored unless the ball has been played or touched by a player-other than the kicker before passing through the goal.

Member: What decisive part does the air force play in a war?

Candidate: The most important part it plays is the strategic bombing of the enemy. We destroy his war material, his aeroplanes and all the bases from where he gets war supplies. The great economic loss inflicted on him often brings him to his knees.

Member: What other functions does it perform during war time?

Mr. Raman: It helps us to carry men and material most quickly to places where they are most wanted. It also helps to throw paratroops behind enemy lines to harass him and cut off his supplies.

Member: What are some of the important components of an air defence system?

Mr. Raman: We should have a chain of an early warning radar system at strategic points to give warning of the approach of enemy aircraft, next the ground control interception facilities and fighter aircraft to fight the enemy's fighters and destroy his bombers, etc.

Member: Will these prove sufficient?

Mr. Raman: No Sir, they are only part of a vast system. We must develop an effective system of command, control, and coordination at all levels, so that at the time of emergency everything is in tip-top condition.

Member: What do you understand by Depth Charge?

Mr. Raman: It is a bomb which can be set to detonate at a given depth below the surface of the sea. It is used mainly as an anti-submarine device.

Member: What is a Zeppelin?

Mr. Raman: It was the large air-ship first built in Germany.

Member: And what is Isotherm?

Mr. Raman: It is a line drawn on a map through places having equal temperature.

Member: What is a "Drift"?

Mr. Raman: Sir, this is a term that denotes the motion of an aircraft in a horizontal plane, under the influence of an air current.

Member: On what date did the Second World War begin?

Mr. Raman: The Second World War began on September 1, 1939, when German troops marched into Poland, without any declaration of war.

Member: When did England declare war on Germany?

Mr. Raman: Two days after, *i.e.,* on September 3, 1939, Great Britain and France together declared war on Germany honouring their pledge to defend Polish independence.

Member: When did France fall?

Mr. Raman: The battle of France was almost over when the defence of Paris was abandoned on June 9, 1940. Paris was finally occupied by the Nazis three days after.

Member: When did Nazi armies invade the former USSR?

Mr. Raman: It was on June 22, 1941 that Nazi armies marched into the USSR led by the Nazi Air Force.

Member: What was the Pearl Harbour incident?

Mr. Raman: Pearl Harbour is a US Pacific naval base on Oahu island, an inlet in Hawaii and scene of Japanese attack on December 7, 1941, which took place while Japanese envoys were holding "peace" talks at Washington. Between 150 and 200 Japanese aircraft operating from aircraft carriers did much serious damage to warships and army installations. The local commanders, Admiral Kimmel and Gen. Short, were relieved of their commands but not found guilty of dereliction of duty.

Member: Can you state the various ranks in the Air Force?

Mr. Raman: Yes Sir. The lowest is the pilot, higher to him is the Flying Officer, higher up is the Flying Lieutenant, next in order are Squadron Leader, Wing Commander, Group Captain, Air Commodore, Air-Vice Marshal, Air Marshal, Air Chief Marshal of the Air Force.

Member: What changes have been made in the rank braids of officers of the Indian Air Force after the country's freedom?

Mr. Raman: The rank braids (*i.e.,* the stripes) have remained unchanged but the crown and eagle in the uniform buttons have been replaced by the national emblem. They have now the Ashoka Lions and IAF eagle instead. Similarly, the Crown has been replaced by officers' and airmen's cap-badge and IAF crests.

Chairman: What is the approximate amount of Government spending on the Defence Forces?

Candidate: About 14 per cent of the total expenditure goes to defence.

Chairman: Don't you think it is unnecessarily heavy?

Mr. Raman: Sir, this may be proportionately heavy for a developing country like India, but so long as the fear of war looms, and international tension does not subside and there is no improvement in the relations between our country and Pakistan, we cannot afford to slack off.

Chairman: In which directions would you suggest any economy to be effected?

Mr. Raman: Sir, the Defence Ministry must see to it that no useless purchases are made, the equipment is purchased from reliable firms whose tenders must be sifted by a Committee of Experts, so that contractors do not bribe the officers and get their tenders accepted at more than the fair and competitive or market prices of the goods and keep a strict general watch over purchases and see that there are no duplications and purchase of unnecessary items.

Chairman: Do you suggest reduction in the forces also?

Mr. Raman: Sir, whereas I would like inefficient officers or such men in the ranks to be eliminated, I would not advocate false economy to endanger the security of the country. It is for the experts to decide how much should be the strength of the army to safeguard the country from dangers, both external and internal.

Chairman: All right Mr. Raman you can go now.

Mr. Raman: Thank you Sir.

> **Comments:** *The candidate is acquainted with knowledge of various fields. He reveals self-confidence and optimism and faces new challenges with resourcefulness, courage and determination.*

Model Interview for Merchant Navy Services

Model Interview-20

Mr. Krishna Moorthy is a handsome young studying boy, qualified for Merchant Navy interview and called for. He is full of enthusiasm and energy of success. With his pleasant personality and good academic record he enters the interview hall and greets the members along with the chairman.

The Interview

Mr. Moorthy: Good Morning to you all Sirs.

Chairman: Good Morning Mr. Moorthy, please take your seat.

Mr. Moorthy: Thank you Sir (*after taking seat*).

Chairman: Where are you studying at present?

Mr. Moorthy: At Ramjas College, Delhi.

Chairman: What attracts you to the Merchant Navy?

Mr. Moorthy: Sir, I like to have a career in the Merchant Navy because life in it is very attractive, to see new places, visit foreign lands and enlarge one's circle of friends. Every year our naval ships go abroad on cruises. We are thus not only able to see new places and people, but we have also the honour of being the unofficial ambassadors of India and of being the messengers of India's goodwill.

Chairman: What are the Gallantry Awards given by the Indian Government for distinguished service in the Indian Army?

Mr. Moorthy: They are: Param Vir Chakra, Maha Vir Chakra, Vir Chakra and Ashok Chakra. The last one is conferred in recognition of acts other than those in combat with the enemy as for example in maintaining law and order.

Member: Which are the natural harbours of India?

Mr. Moorthy: Cochin and Visakhapatnam are the natural harbours of India. They are free India's major ports.

Member: Where did the German Navy surrender to the British in the First Great War?

Mr. Moorthy: At Scappa Flow on the east coast of Scotland, Sir.

Member: What incident do you connect with that surrender?

Mr. Moorthy: The Germans scuttled their ships as they entered the port.

Member: How do ships at sea signal to each other?

Mr. Moorthy: By flags and radio.

Member: What was Nelson's famous signal at the Battle of Trafalgar?

Mr. Moorthy: "England expects every man to do his duty".

Member: With which other countries, besides Britain, does Indian Merchant Navy have valuable contacts?

Mr. Moorthy: With Japan, Egypt and the Persian Gulf ports, etc.

Member: Which is the most important naval dockyard in the East?

Mr. Moorthy: Singapore is the largest; it is a floating dock.

Member: What gives it so much importance?

Mr. Moorthy: Because it serves as a watch-post in the Indian Ocean. It commands entrance to the Far-East and has, therefore, been made a strong base by the British.

Member: But why could they not hold it against the Japanese in the Second World-War?

Mr. Moorthy: This was because the Japanese attacked it through the mainland. Whoever holds the Malaysian mainland, can easily hold Singapore.

Member: What other importance has Singapore?

Mr. Moorthy: It has developed into a very important entrepot, serves Malaysia and exports large quantities of tin, rubber and copper.

Member: When was the Spanish Armada defeated by the British Navy?

Mr. Moorthy: I don't remember the year, Sir, but this Armada was defeated by Drake.

Member: The Spanish Armada was defeated in the year 1588.

Candidate: Thank you, Sir.

Member: Where does the American Navy chiefly operate?

Mr. Moorthy: Two-thirds of the American Navy is distributed along the Atlantic sea-board of the USA and one-third in the Pacific Waters.

Member: With which section of the British Defence Forces is the name of the Lord Louis Mountbatten associated?

Mr. Moorthy: With Royal Navy, Sir.

Member: Have, you read any poem whose theme is the gallantry of a naval officer's son in the performance of his duty?

Mr. Moorthy: Yes Sir. It is the poem, Casabianca.

Member: What is meant by the expression "Freedom of the seas"?

Mr. Moorthy: This refers to the peaceful conditions of trade enjoyed by the merchant navies of the world, in the seven seas made possible in former days by the protection afforded by the British Navy.

Member: Which was the greatest naval power in 17th century?

Mr. Moorthy: Spain was the greatest naval power.

Member: What do you understand by the phrase "Twelve-mile limit" ?

Mr. Moorthy: It is an expression referring to the twelve-mile or 19 km expanses of water out from any shore, the jurisdiction over which belongs to the country owning the mainland. This is called the territorial waters.

Chairman: What is a destroyer?

Mr. Moorthy: Sir, it is a kind of battleship which has 4 to 8 guns mounted on it and a number of torpedo tubes. It is used to protect convoys.

Chairman: Has India built some destroyers?

Mr. Moorthy: Yes sir, India has now built quite a number of destroyers, though, she purchased some of those from the British Navy and renamed these as INS Rana, INS Rajput and INS Ranjit.

Chairman: What are the new designs for the crests and badges of our ships and establishments?

Mr. Moorthy: Sir, the Tudor Crown and Star of India have now been replaced by the Ashok Pedestal and the Lotus respectively in the badges and crests of Indian Naval Ships and establishments.

Chairman: Why has it been thought better to have the laurel of lotus buds in place of the old star of India?

Mr. Moorthy: Because the laurel of lotus has been India's national floral symbol for centuries. Also as it symbolises creation out of water, it is one of the most popular motif used in ancient and modern Indian Art.

Chairman: Thank you, Mr. Moorthy, you can go now.

> ***Comments:*** *The candidate is fully acknowledged with his subject of study. Along with that, he is acquainted with latest development around him. He displays a confident personality with determination.*

Model Interview for Combined Graduate Level Exam

Model Interview-21

Mr. Prabin Kumar Sharma, graduated in Zoology. He is now pursuing M.Sc. in Zoology from B.N. Mandal University,

Madhepura. Mr. Sharma reaches the venue well-dressed in a spotless cream-coloured shirt with a fountain pen visible in his pocket. He waits curiously for his turn. When called, he moves towards the interview room with confident steps. He pushes the door open and seeks for permission.

The Interview

Prabin: May I come in, Sir?

Chairman: Yes, come in.

Prabin: Good afternoon, madam. Good afternoon, Sirs.

Chairman: Good afternoon, be seated, please.

Prabin: Thank you, Sir.

[Mr. Prabin sits down softly in the chair without making any noticeable noise. He is quite relaxed and ready for the query from the board]

Chairman: Are you Prabin Sharma?

Prabin: Yes, Sir.

Chairman: What is your date of birth?

Prabin: It is 3rd January 19..., Sir.

Chairman: Where have you come from?

Prabin: Sir, I am a resident of Bihar?

Chairman: What is Dilawarganj?

Prabin: Sir, it is the name of my village where I live.

Chairman: How did you come here?

Prabin: I came by train, Sir.

Chairman: Was the train journey long?

Prabin: Sir, it took me 10 hours to reach here?

Chairman: What is the distance between Kishanganj and Kolkata?

Prabin: It is 483 km long, Sir.

First Member: You had Zoology in your B.Sc. (Hons.) course?

Prabin: Yes Sir.

First Member: Then, what are you doing now?

Prabin: I am doing M.Sc. (Zoology), Sir.

Lady Member: From which University?

Prabin: From B.N. Mandal University, Madhepura, madam.

Chairman: What?

Prabin: Sir, Bhupendra Narayan Mandal University, Madhepura.

First Member: Normal pulse rate ranges 70-90 per minute, 70/min in man and 80/min in women. Tell me, what is cardiac cycle?

Prabin: The cycle of events occurred in single heart beat is called cardiac cycle. A cardiac cycle takes about 0.8 second.

First Member: Very good, which blood can be given to anyone and why?

Prabin: Group O blood can be given to anyone. It is without antigens.

First Member: Very good, what is the Rh-system?

Prabin: The Rhesus (Rh) system is the most important of the other blood group systems. It was discovered by Landsteiner and Weiner in 1940. If an individual's red cells were agglutinated by this antiserum, they were said to have the Rhesus factor on their red cells (*i.e.,* Rh positive). If an individual's cells were not agglutinated by the antiserum, they were said to lack the Rhesus factor (*i.e.,* Rh negative).

First Member: Which species of fish carries its eggs in a pouch in the male's body?

Prabin: Sir, the sea horse. (Hippocampus hippocampus)

First Member: Very good, besides being a bird, what else is a Kiwi?

Prabin: Sir, a fruit.

First Member: The nickname given to the New Zealand cricket team is the same as that of a flightless bird. Name it.

Prabin: Sir. The Kiwi.

First Member: For studying the communication aspect of which insect was Karl Von Frisch awarded the 1973 Nobel Prize for Physiology or Medicine?

Prabin: Sir, the honey bees.

First Member: Very good. How many times does a bee bite?

Prabin: Only once. Sir.

First Member: What is the difference between a pigeon and a dove?

Prabin: Sir, there is no difference.

First Member: Which specific branch of zoology deals with the study of fishes?

Prabin: Sir, Ichthyology.

First Member: How would a student of botany classify a tomato and a brinjal?

Prabin: Sir, as forms of berries.

First Member: What is the rate at which fingernails grow?

Prabin: Sir, I may be wrong but I do think that roughly the rate at which fingernails grow is about 1 cm to 10 cm every year.

First Member: Comment on Octopus.

Prabin: Octopus is a marine nocturnal deep sea form found at the bottom of the sea. It feeds on crabs, fishes, and other molluscs. It has colour changing habit. It can crawl by its arm and can also swim backwards by ejecting jet of water from the funnel.

First Member: Very good, why do rats gnaw?

Prabin: Sir, rats have one pair of sharp chisel-like incisors in each jaw. When these teeth grow to the maximum length, they disturb the rats in opening and closing their mouth. Thus they gnaw so that teeth may reduce to the proper size.

First Member: O.K., tell me, which vitamin is responsible for yellow colour of ripen mango?

Prabin: Sir, vitamin 'C'.

Chairman: Have you read 'the Constitution'?

Prabin: Yes Sir.

Second Member: Who was the chairman of the Drafting Committee?

Prabin: Dr. B.R. Ambedkar

Second Member: Expand B.R.

Prabin: Sir, Bhimrao Ramji.

Chairman: Explain Fundamental Duties.

Prabin : The 42nd constitutional amendment act has inserted part IVA with Article 51A having a set of fundamental duties. There are 10 fundamental duties which have been mentioned in Indian Constitution, according to which, it shall be the duty of every citizen of India to obey the constitution and respect its ideals, institution and the National anthem and the National flag and to safeguard public property and to abjure violence.

Chairman: Something more.....

Prabin: To protect the sovereignty, unity and integrity. To develop the scientific temper, humanism and the spirit of inquiry and reform.

Second Member: How is your knowledge of English?

Prabin: Sir, I am quite good at English vocabulary which is particularly required for office work.

Second Member: Have you got any knowledge of computer?

Prabin: Yes Sir. I have got 6 month's CIC course.

Second Member: What is CIC ?

Prabin: Sir, Certificate in Computing.

Chairman: Differentiate between direct and indirect taxes.

Prabin: Sir, a tax is said to be a direct tax when it is not intended to be shifted to anybody else. Indirect tax is that tax which is levied on goods or services produced or purchased. Indirect taxes are demanded from one person in the expectation and intention that he shall indemnify himself at the expense of another.

Chairman: Is income tax an indirect tax?

Prabin: No Sir, Income Tax is an example of direct tax.

Chairman: Why in your opinion many people do not file an income-tax return?

Prabin: In my opinion, most of such people are quite honest but they do not file an income-tax return because they fear that they would be harassed by the Income-Tax Department if they do so.

Lady Member: Name the TV Programmes which you watch?

Prabin: Madam, I watch "Earth Matters" on DD-1.

Lady Member: You have mentioned writing poems as your hobby in your Bio Data.

Prabin: Yes, Madam.

Lady Member: Which type of poems do you compose?

Prabin: Madam, I compose poems on Nature and fair sexes.

Lady Member: Which type of books do you read?

Prabin: I prefer non-fiction.

Lady Member: Why?

Prabin: It strengthens various areas of knowledge. It influences on my mind and soul positively.

Lady Member: Does fiction not have such influences?

Prabin: No, madam. Fictions are written by scholars. Author's experiences and experiments on society are reflected in their works. What we read in fictions is nothing but fruits of the best endeavours of authors. Both fiction and non-fiction are the work of creativity. But, it is my liking. I do not have a taste in characters.

Lady Member: What is the book that you have read last?

Prabin: *The Theory of Everything* by Stephen W. Hawking.

Chairman: All right, Mr. Prabin Sharma, you can go now.

Prabin: Thank you Sir.

> **Comment:** *The candidate is fully acknowledged with his subject of study. Along with that, he is acquainted with latest development around him. He displays a confident personality with determination.*

Model Interview for Managerial Service (MBA)

Model Interview-22

Priyanshu Rajan is a tough built youngman with fair height and medium complexion. He looks impressive and handsome. His movements are measured and relaxed indicating rhythm, poise and self-confidence. His face displays warmth and cheerful smile. When called for an interview, he enters the room and greets all the members of the board.

The Interview

Mr. Rajan: Good Morning, you all Sirs.

Member: Good Morning Mr. Rajan, please take your seat.

Mr. Rajan: Thank you, Sir.

Member: You were in Military service and adjoined with Press why?

Mr. Rajan: Yes Sir, after class 12th I had joined the Military service. That time I had needed a way to pay for my further studies. Also for patriotic reason and because I wanted some adventure before I settle down, I had also keen desire to live in connection with people through press. So I used to write news and articles for public, workers and others.

Member: Why do you want to leave the Military service?

Mr. Rajan: I am leaving the military service because I am not being developed to my full potential. I like the people and the organisation. I am ready to move on to bigger challenges.

Member: What would you bring to this company?

Mr. Rajan: The primary motivation of the military is readiness with the ability to wage war. Every decision I made had that objective in mind even though it sometimes conflicted with my personal goals or other individual goal. General Robert Wood Johnson's credo is : Customers, Employees, Community and Stockholders. The primary motivation of your organisation is to create maximum long term wealth for the company owners. I would find sound analytical solutions and build enthusiasm with the people, I work with to implement the solutions that achieves that credo.

Member: What kind of work are you looking for?

Mr. Rajan: I am looking for a job that will challenge me each day. I enjoy interacting with people, and when appropriate, I like to help them solve problems. I also want to grow professionally and be paid appropriately for my success.

Member: Give me an example of when you motivated a group?

Mr. Rajan: As the repair parts chief of a new logistics headquarters, I motivated my new team to perform its best. We had the quickest start and the fewest problems. I did this by establishing the values and setting direction and goals. I then lead by example becoming a subject matter expert in my field and being on the floor. People respect that.

Member: Tell me what you would do if you could not motivate someone?

Mr. Rajan: Sometimes there are personal problems, which distract folks. I believe people are good and want to do a good job. If a person has a problem, I help them solve it. As a last resort, I would assist them in finding employment elsewhere, because my company will not be a welfare organization.

Member: How do you feel about unions?

Mr. Rajan: Unions were established to protect the individual worker. I think that sometimes they lose sight of that goal. I can work with them though. The way that Army officers deal with individual soldiers is quite similar.

Member: How do you feel about shift work?

Mr. Rajan: I am open. I can take advantage of the off time to pursue other interests outside of work.

Member: If I asked your last supervisor what your greatest asset was, what would they say?

Mr. Rajan: I don't know Sir. I give 100% effort and don't leave anything left undone when the day is over. I can get rather passionate about my work, as I believe everyone should.

Member: What happens when you must start an unpopular program?

Mr. Rajan: I think the most important aspect of implementing an unpopular program is setting the example. When I implement an unpopular program, I explain its significance in terms of its objectives and how they relate to the company values. I then set the example.

Member: Would you list some of the significant economic steps of recent times?

Mr. Rajan: A realistic tax structure and reduced maximum rate of income tax.

Member: What is realistic in it?

Mr. Rajan: Those having annual incomes upto ₹ 1,50,000 have been exempted and the maximum rate of taxation has been brought down considerably. It is a maximum of 30% plus 10% surcharge on total income exceeding Rs. five lakh per annum.

Member: But how does that become realistic?

Mr. Rajan: The temptation to evade taxes has definitely been weakened.

Member: What do you mean? Do you think the Government cannot introduce another Voluntary Disclosure of Income Scheme?

Mr. Rajan: *(affably)* I don't think that would be necessary. The Income Tax Department has been sufficiently greared up to maintain a constant and effective check.

Member: What type of economy have we got here in India?

Mr. Rajan: It is a Mixed Economy.

Member: Do you think that is the best we could have?

Mr. Rajan: *(with confidence)* Definitely yes, Sir.

Member: Why not an absolutely free or controlled economy?

Mr. Rajan: I don't think, Sir, an absolutely free or totally controlled economy is possible in practice in this country.

Member: How about the USA?

Mr. Rajan: As far as I know, even their economy is not absolutely free. Certain amount of Government interference is there.

Member: But don't you think a mixed economy gets messy at times?

Mr. Rajan: *(appearing to agree)* Only at times, Sir.

Member: But that could be any time?

Mr. Rajan: I see nothing to be afraid of, Sir. The Government is armed with sufficient powers to deal with any type of situation.

(Silence... some members are scribbling)

Chairman: Will you name any five public sector undertakings?

Mr. Rajan: *(trying to recollect)* Bharat Heavy Electricals, Cement Corporation of India (CCI)...

Chairman : *(intervening)* What is this CCI doing?

Mr. Rajan: It is manufacturing cement.

Chairman: Is it in competition with the private sector?

Mr. Rajan: Yes, Sir. But it is not a perfect competition.

Chairman: How do you say that?

Mr. Rajan: CCI manufactures cement on a large scale. The private sector is also manufacturing it but on a small scale. Thus, CCI enjoys a basic cost advantage.

Member: That way, in case they come to dominate the market what would you call them?

Mr. Rajan: That will tend towards monopoly.

Member: How do you describe a market which is dominated by a few people?

Mr. Rajan: An oligopoly.

Member: And if the market is dominated by a few buyers, what do you call that?

Mr. Rajan: *(wiping his brow)* Sorry, Sir, I do not know.

Chairman: Suppose you have to raise a share capital of ₹ 1 crore. Would you go straight to the share market?

Mr. Rajan: *(looking relieved)* No, Sir. I shall have to seek the permission of the Controller of Capital Issues first.

Chairman: Why was this Controller of Capital Issues Act passed?

Mr. Rajan: Under the Indian Companies Act, 1956, every limited company is entitled to raise capital by public issues of shares. In order to regulate this right and to avoid malpractices, this Act was passed.

Member: *(suddenly)* Well! How do you proceed after you have obtained his permission?

Mr. Rajan: Other formalities will have to be completed.

Member: For instance?

Mr. Rajan: I must see to it that the entire issue is under-written.

Member: Can't you dispense with the under-writing services to reduce the cost?

Mr. Rajan: Sir, I don't think it costs that much when we look at the advantages it has.

Member: What advantages?

Mr. Rajan: One has a sense of security. Prospective shareholders judge the popularity of the issue by that. A reputed under-writer can be of great help.

Member: But won't the buyers look into the company's financial position?

Mr. Rajan: *(with confidence)* Yes, of course. That is the most important thing.

(Chairman nods his head approvingly)

Member: Do you participate in any game. Mr. Rajan?

Mr. Rajan: Yes Sir. I play cricket.

Member: In which department of the game do you excel?

Mr. Rajan: I am a fast bowler, Sir.

Member: Good. In which other games are you interested?
Candidate: I am interested in all sports.

Member: What do you think of India's performance at the Olympics?

Mr. Rajan: It is poor, Sir.

Member: *(as if outraged)* Poor you say? It was shameful. Look at what a small country like South Korea has been able to accomplish?

Mr. Rajan: But, if you will excuse me, Sir, the comparison is not fair.

Member: Why? Are we to concede that the others are supermen?

Mr. Rajan: *(protesting)* Not at all, Sir. But look at the money and effort they put into developing sports.

Member: We may not be able to afford that sort of expense.

Mr. Rajan: Obviously in that case we should adopt a different strategy.

Member: For instance?

Mr. Rajan: We should make sports a part of school and college curricula, spot talent and do all we can to bring it up to international standards.

Chairman: *(with a smile)* It's all right Mr. Rajan. Thank you very much.

Mr. Rajan: *(rising)* Thank you, Sir.

> ***Comment:*** *The candidate is intelligent and well-informed. He displays awareness regarding the latest developments. He is able to decide the priorities with speed and accuracy and knows how to utilize the resources at his disposal to ensure optimum results.*

Chapter 8

Post Interview

When an interview is over, one is not sure whether he will get the job offer or not. But without thinking of result of interview one should send a follow-up letter/letter of thanks to the company. One should understand the value and power of a 'thank you' letter. A 'thank you note' freshens the memory of your candidacy in the employer's mind. One should never forget to send a letter of thanks at the earliest, if sent late it loses its meaning. The letter may be either typed or handwritten on plain paper. It should be formal, professional and precise. It works as a powerful tool. Sample follow-up letter is:

Deepak Sharma
M.G. Road
Ranchi

20 May, 20...

Mr. (Name of Interviewer)

Job Title ....

Name of company

Add ....

....

Sir,

I would like to convey my sincere thanks to you for all the very congenial cooperation extended during my interview on dated .... for the post of (name of the job/vacant position). I am very much pleased and excited about the prospect of joining the ABC company and working with the great team of achievers. The way I was interviewed was indeed very encouraging.

My exposure, experience and knowledge indeed match best with the necessity of the vacant post. If there is any need of any information please call me on this number .... anytime.

I am waiting for a positive response from you.

With Thanks!

Your's sincerely

Deepak Sharma

After completion of interview, there is a short discussion on salary.

Here are some salary negotiation tips that will work for you and help you bargain your way to a fair salary.

Salary Negotiation Tips

- The most important thing to remember when discussing your salary is that it is a negotiation. Like any form of bartering, the first figure you mention in the job interview probably won't be the figure you agree on. But it's a place to start.

- Be confident about what you're worth. Recognise that you're bringing something unique to the Company, and that you're worth the wage you're requesting. Even if you've only just finished school or college, you still have something unique to offer and it's important to bear that in mind as you think about salary negotiation.

- Remember also that it's not easy finding the right person for a job. If you've impressed the interviewers enough to employ you, you have the upper hand and paying a little more to keep you isn't too big a deal.

  So ask for a slightly higher salary than you expect.

- If the job advertisement mentions a salary range, employers will be prepared to pay more for the right candidate. If you're a little uncomfortable asking for the top figure, choose one just above the mid-range. This gives the impression that you are worth a good wage and is a great place to start.

Assuming an advertised salary range of ₹ 1,30,000 to ₹ 1,42,000, you might say this:

"I'm expecting a salary in the region of ₹ 1,38,000, based on my knowledge and experience."

- Remember that salary is not everything. If the salary is less than you hoped and the Company won't or can't go any higher, ask about other benefits which are important to you like training courses, financial help with further study and so on.

- If salary is the most important factor in your decision to accept a job, we recommend a little more reading on the subject before your interview.

Visit Internet for a number of good books on salary negotiation.

For a small price, they can give you a big lead.

Chapter 9

Learning from Failure

Setbacks are necessary to make character strong. Each time you overcome a failure, you emerge stronger. Every trial exhausts some form of error. No attempt is a complete failure. No failure is without some benefit.

Due to mistakes, one has to face failure. If one thinks that he has burnt all his boats, he goes in depression and gets mentally paralysed. If one looks upon it as a temporary setback, he rises above it. Such a person looks upon failure as a challenge, and an opportunity.

Failure is a training ground. Our greatest glory is not in never failing, but in rising after every fall. Greatness lies, not in avoiding failures, but in overpowering them. Every failure leaves you a little more confident. In time of stress and strain, there is tendency to lean on others. That tendency cripples your capacity to overcome difficulties and obstacles.

One can learn from his failure. He should think about his mistakes, about his wrong attitude, that he has done in prior try, and he should try his best not to repeat those mistakes again. Failure and self-thoughtfulness on its reason and result gives strength for struggle.

Think of the mighty struggle of a seed to sprout from the earth's bosom into a mighty oak!

You resemble a tiny seed. You have the potential to grow into formidable proportions hidden within you. If you will come under pressure and give up the struggle needed for flowering, you wither away into nothingness. If you grow half your strength, one whiff of a gale will uproot you. It will twist you into a lifeless twig. If you have grown to your full potential and learnt to bend with the storms, you will stand the test of adversity.

Success comes after wrestling with insurmountable obstacles and failures. Don't lose your faith in yourself, however heartbreaking the failure. Faith is life's greatest asset. It gives hope and confidence and the will to carry through impossible situations.

There is only need of your attitude to see the failure. You must face failure realistically, as something to prove your mettle. A failure is an opportunity to prove how strong you are. The number of times you try is not important, the important consideration is the intelligence with which you try, and above all what you yourself discover from tries.

Chapter 10

Important Tips for Interview

An interview can make or break you, so take your personality development rather seriously and make sure to attend some mock interviews at leading institutes.

- The first thing you need to do prior to interviewing is assess yourself. This includes listing your strengths and weaknesses, accomplishments and achievements, reviewing strong and weak point and recording some of the key decisions you have made in your life.

- Review your interests, the disappointments you've encountered, your work environment likes/dislikes, your business and personal values, your goals, needs, restrictions and lifestyle preferences. It would help if you are ready to practice answering the following potential questions.

- There are generally 5/6 members at the interview board with the chairperson. Enter the room confidently and greet the chairperson and pleasantly nod at other members. Wait till you are asked to sit.

- Intelligent listening is the mantra, and for this maintaining eye contact is very important. Your posture should be attentive and relaxed.

- Cut your answer short to the required patience shown by the member talking to you. They usually like to talk more, so listen carefully and think for a few seconds before you start answering the question. This will show that you are organising your thoughts in mind before starting to speak.

- Leave some room for difference in opinion. Do take a stand, but do not look adamant or unwilling to appreciate the board's opinion.

- Use couple of words from the questions while answering any question. It shows you have listened to the questions very carefully, and you are serious about it all.

- Have a knack for both essentials and minute details.

- Remember that interviewer will see through everything to assess whether you can really take up the reins.

- Since the personality characteristics are adjudged on the basis of your views, ideas and responses, try to form your own in-depth analysis of men and matters.

- Try to handle delicate and controversial issues with commendable tact, resourcefulness, and persuasiveness. Never take a rigid stand, but be free, frank and bold to express your views.

- Keep yourself up to date with the world around you and make your own analysis of every branch of activity from political, social and economic to cultural and scientific.

- You should be serious about your career and the interview, but excessive obsession breeds fear and nervousness mars your prospects. When you raise an argument, strengthen it with all the facts you can marshal.

○○○